DINGLE

D I N G L E

Dinners

**From the Chefs
of Ireland's
#1 Foodie Town**

TREVIS L. GLEASON is a member of the organising committee for the Dingle Food Festival, Ambassador for the Blas na hÉireann awards, a founding judge of the Irish Quality Food Awards and has been an award-winning culinarian and instructor at such institutions as Cornell University, New England Culinary Institute and California Culinary Academy. His memoir, *Chef Interrupted*, won the Prestige Award at the Gourmand World Cookbook Awards. He lives with MS and runs Life With MS, a widely read and respected blog, as well as giving regular talks about living life fully. He lives in Seattle, Washington, and Dingle with his wife, Caryn, and their two Wheaten Terriers, Sadie and Maggie.

Stay up to date with Trevis at:

www.trevislgleason.com

www.facebook.com/LifeWithMS

@TrevisGleason

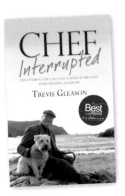

Gourmand International
World Cookbook
Award Winner

Dedicated to the memory of
Oliver Hughes and Owen Kane

Two men of vision, taste and appetite
who loved Dingle, its people and
its produce. They endeavoured,
with great success, to enhance its
international gastronomic reputation.

DINGLE

Dinners

〰

**From the Chefs
of Ireland's
#1 Foodie Town**

Compiled and edited by

TREVIS L. GLEASON

Foreword by
NEVEN MAGUIRE

The Collins Press

First published in 2017 by
The Collins Press
West Link Park
Doughcloyne
Wilton
Cork
T12 N5EF
Ireland

A CIP record for this book is available from the British Library.

Hardback ISBN: 978-1-84889-328-3

Profile photography by Elaine Kennedy (www.elainekennedy.com)
Food and prop styling by Jette Virdi (www.jettevirdi.com)
Food Photography by Joanne Murphy (www.joanne-murphy.com)
Cover design by Fidelma Slattery

Design and typesetting by Studio 10 Design
Typeset in Athelas and Franklin Gothic

Printed in Spain by LiberDúplex

Cover photographs
Front: Glenbeigh oysters with marsh samphire, from Oysters Casino by Trevis L. Gleason (see p. 52)
Back: *(top)* Mami's Beef Goulash by Maja Beaujouan, The Little Cheese Shop (see p. 104); *(centre)* Crab and Dingle Whiskey Bisque by Martin Bealin, The Global Village (see p. 83); *(bottom)* Dingle Whiskey and Sherry Trifle by Pat Moore, Beginish (see p. 36).

With the kind support of the Dingle Whiskey Distillery and the Dingle Food Festival

CONTENTS

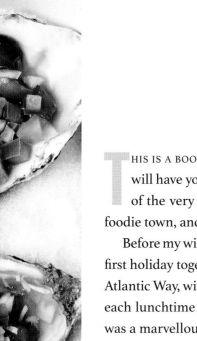

FOREWORD

by Neven Maguire

THIS IS A BOOK to bring back wonderful memories, and its pictures and recipes will have you looking at the diary for dates to visit Dingle and call in at some of the very finest places to eat in Ireland. Dingle is deservedly known as a foodie town, and Trevis L. Gleason's book has all the essential signposts.

Before my wife Amelda and I were married, Dingle was where we went for our first holiday together. I remember the days cycling on what we now call the Wild Atlantic Way, with its spectacular scenery. We stayed in some excellent B&Bs and each lunchtime and evening we treated ourselves to some memorable meals. It was a marvellous holiday during the first flush of love. We have been back often since then and always know there will be a warm welcome and wonderful food. I enjoyed a great demo at the Dingle Food Festival and I also enjoyed my time there as a judge for Blas na hÉireann. Dingle has so many good food producers to celebrate and plenty of fine products make their way into my larder in Blacklion, County Cavan. People often ask me what my essentials are. Well, I will never be without a good Irish rapeseed oil, some Irish sea salt and several infused balsamic vinegars.

Cooking at home is one of my great pleasures. From the beginning, my young twins have eaten what Amelda and I eat. It's interesting now to see them wanting to get involved in cooking. They learn so much at this age that will stand to them. They are learning how to shop for food and I trust that they are also learning that eating together, tasting food that you have bought locally or grown in your own garden and cooked in your own kitchen is one of life's great pleasures. The French and Italians have understood this for generations, but we were in danger of letting it slip away. However, I think the tide is turning back. As a family, we will usually cook something simple, like grilled Killybegs hake with lovely potatoes and fresh vegetables. Another favourite is a Cavan corn-fed chicken poached in a vegetable and barley soup.

Travelling the country for my RTÉ television series, I have seen how Irish food has been improving in leaps and bounds, and Dingle will always be a jewel in the crown. I look forward to trying some of the recipes from these great chefs and Amelda and I look forward to our next family visit to the wonderful restaurants featured within these pages.

INTRODUCTION

'**A** Fruit and Veg Man, a Fisherman and a Baggage Guy board a train in Dublin.' Hand to God, this is how this book began.

It was 18 July 2015 and I had just finished judging the finals of the Irish Quality Food Awards in Dublin. My wife and I found that our seats on the train home to Kerry were across the aisle from three middle-aged mischievants headed to Killarney for the replay of the Munster GAA football championship. Though they tried to pass themselves off as simple working-class men of humble employment, the quality of their shoes and the food they'd brought aboard gave them away (one betrayed them to my wife, the other to me). You can't take someone for a football rowdy when they're wearing €300 shoes and snacking on doughnut peaches, oak-smoked wild salmon and a stick of chorizo that a pilot friend had brought back for the Baggage Guy on a flight from Spain.

We eventually learned that the Fruit and Veg Man was the owner of a large produce distributor, the Fisherman was a seafood wholesaler with a medium-sized fleet of fishing boats and the Baggage Guy was the director of ground crew at Dublin's international airport. Just three old Dublin friends headed down to watch some really good football in what ended up being a torrential downpour that saw Kerry defeat Cork 1–11 to 1–6 to take the Munster Senior Football Cup.

When the conversation finally got around to why two Yanks were heading to Kerry, I think they expected to hear something about holidays and sightseeing. When we told them that we lived in Kerry, they were intrigued.

They asked why we had decided to shift our lives from Seattle to Kerry. We answered with our pat answer – 'Living the dream while we can' – and they laughed while hiding their bottle of imported Normandy cider from the conductor passing to check for tickets. Owing to their deftness at concealing the contraband, I was thinking that our three might have had a joyfully raucous past indeed.

When we told the trio that we lived in Dingle, well, that's when they changed.

Their faces split into childlike grins as they recalled times and places along the peninsula they'd visited together or with their families. They nearly cooed about the rugged terrain, from the sacred peak of Mount Brandon to the sandy strands that dot our townlands. The real excitement, however, came when they started talking about the food.

They not only recited the names of the restaurants and pubs where they had dined, but also those that they intended to visit on their next trip. They knew the names of some of my chef friends who owned or worked in these places. They even knew of some of the speciality shops and purveyors in Dingle.

These lads knew their food and they knew Dingle was a place to get some of the best in the country. Of course, I knew this already, but for three football fans from Dublin to give any praise whatsoever to their arch-rivals in Kerry spoke volumes. And so it was that the seed was planted for the book you now hold.

I sat down with several of the chefs of Dingle to talk about the area, their backgrounds and what brought them to this magical 'island on an island', as the people of west Kerry often refer to the place. They are consummate gentlemen and ladies. They are loveable rakes. They are professional and mischievous, family men and women, married, single and (oft more than once) divorced. These are the hard-working, hard-playing, burnt, bruised, cut and scarred people behind the swinging door who prepare some of the best food Ireland has to offer to diners from near and far.

'Ye are very welcome', as they say in west Kerry, to enjoy the menus and recipes these chefs cook for their families, colleagues and friends when (or, as some of them pointed out, if) they have a free afternoon and a few bottles of wine. These are not the foods that you'll see on the menus of the chef's hotels and restaurants: they are the meals shared at their own tables and we all hope you will enjoy them on yours.

Cheers
TLG
2017

THE CHEFS

DURING A COLD AND BLUSTERY west Kerry winter 'off-season', I sat down with twenty-five remarkable chefs of Dingle, County Kerry – voted Ireland's first #1 Foodie Town in 2014. Over cups of tea or coffee (and sometimes a pint) we talked about where they came from, why they came to Dingle and what made them stay.

This was not conversation about what foods owners or customers demanded from them but, rather, the foods they like to cook and eat at home. Not the menus you'll see if you enter the respected restaurants and hotels where they serve as leading cooks, but the menu they'd offer to friends and to family on the rare occasion they have a dinner party of their own.

These are often renditions of food memories from mother's kitchen or brought back from favourite holiday travel. Some are simple and some are bold. Some will test your skills while others will test your nerve. I am sure that whatever menu you choose for your next dinner party, your guests will be happy you did.

You'll note some chef's techniques scattered here and there that we bring home from our professional lives. Whether it's braising meats a day or two in advance or using a smoky barbeque fire to simulate a wood-burning oven, I hope that you'll find the tips and methods in these pages something you'll use in cooking other recipes as well.

We settled on menus for a party of six people for all the recipes, but everyone's appetite is different and you may have a few leftovers – oh, the horror of it.

As we are fortunate here to have the Dingle Whiskey Distillery in our town, you'll note that the chefs are not shy about using their Dingle Original Gin, Dingle Distillery vodka and a few variations of Dingle whiskey in their recipes. I have also paired cocktails using their products with most of the menus. The same goes for beers that might have been used in recipes or as beverage suggestions. We have two very good breweries here and the Porterhouse (parent of the Distillery) brew some fine beers and ales as well.

So, please allow me to introduce you to the chefs of Ireland's #1 Foodie Town…

JOHN RYAN

Dingle Skellig Hotel

AT THE HELM

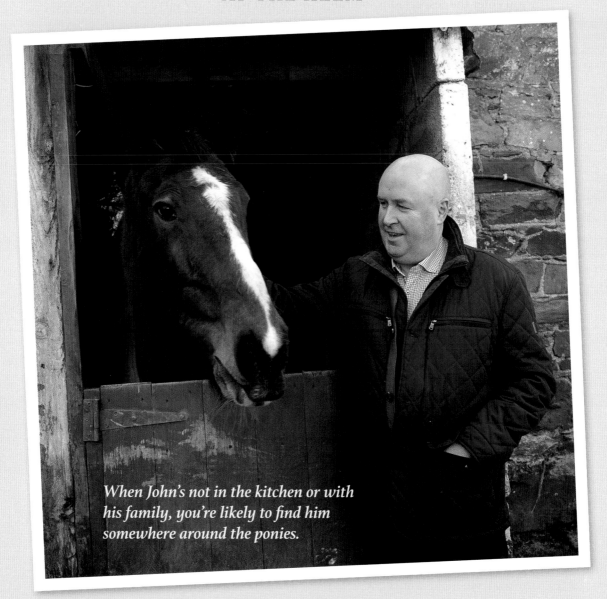

When John's not in the kitchen or with his family, you're likely to find him somewhere around the ponies.

BEGIN where many of the chefs of the Dingle Peninsula whom I interviewed for this book began: at the Dingle Skellig Hotel. For many years, the Skellig, as we call the local standard-bearer for weddings and special occasions, was the busiest place on the peninsula and one of the busiest in the county when it came to training and employing chefs.

At the helm of this venerated property's kitchens since 2010 is a Limerick native, John Ryan. Every fortnight or so, depending on the season, Chef Ryan leaves his wife and three boys and gets under way like a cruise ship captain headed to sea with a boatload of passengers with high expectations and long memories. As well as working at the launching pad for countless culinary careers, like many of those who have worked in the Skellig's kitchens, John made the rounds of the world's culinary centres before dropping anchor in Dingle.

When interviewing many of the chefs in my town, I found that I had worked with some of the same people in our younger years. In this case it was Chef Robert Barral, who had been John's head chef when he was a young cook working on the opening team, based out of Boston, for the Four Seasons Hotels. Chef Robert was the executive chef of the New England Culinary Institute in Vermont, USA, when I was a student there.

Perhaps because he was the oldest of seven children or maybe because of his deep love of children, like many Irish chefs the balance of home, family and work is very important to John. He left a head chef job in the Boston area for London just to be closer to his siblings. 'I got tired of not seeing my brothers and sisters,' he told me when I asked why he moved from Boston to London, where one of his sisters was living. It's probably also one of the reasons he chose the family-friendly menu that he has proffered for this book.

When he goes home to Limerick he spends as much time as possible with his wife and boys – mostly young men now, really. The same goes for when the family comes down to Dingle for summers and holidays. His youngest son doesn't remember a time when Daddy lived at home full-time, which is yet another reason to keep his menu simple and fun for the boys and their friends so that he can take full advantage of the time he does spend with family.

To listen to this Dublin-born (though his family moved before he was one year old) Limerick man praise our small Kerry town the way he does makes me wonder who he shouts for on Sunday afternoons, when GAA football shines bright no matter what the marine weather forecast is like in Dingle. The people, the ingredients, the scenery, the general mood, the quality of life in the place – he can't say enough about the town where he works and lives three quarters of his time.

He tries to walk three or four miles each morning before heading to the hotel for the day. He runs into many of the same faces, many of them 'blow-ins' just like him. He supposes that working for a family-run hotel is part of what makes his life in Dingle worth being separated from his family.

John treats his staff like family as much as possible as well. Like him, many of his senior staff are from Limerick and most of his employees have been with him for almost his entire tenure. He also takes on a couple of culinary students every year and hires local schoolchildren on their summer holidays to give newcomers a leg-up into the industry. Like many eldest children, he takes his responsibility to his family – both his home and his work family – seriously. His passion for looking after his staff is obvious and notable.

John is humble in telling his part of the Skellig story, but he works hard to show off his staff and the hotel at the same time. He is proud of the respect for the quality of food available in Dingle.

'You wouldn't get two or three restaurants of the quality we have here in Dingle if you looked in a city like Limerick.' So when he goes home to Limerick for the weekend, he heads to his local butcher to collect some handy ingredients and puts together a handmade pizza party for his boys and some of their friends. Everyone gets what they want, everyone gets plenty to eat and like his customers – be they hotel guests, wedding parties or families on holiday – everyone goes home happy.

Whether you make this menu for the kids and cousins or as part of a game-day buffet, you'll find yourself coming back to these simple, fun recipes over and over. Make a few bases and offer guests a choice of toppings. For a more adult bent to the party, try Pat Moore's whiskey and sherry trifle (page 36) for the pudding.

HOMEMADE PIZZA PARTY FOR THE FAMILY

starter
BBQ chicken wings
Meatballs in tomato and mushroom fondue
Baked sweet potato wedges

main
Homemade pizza

dessert
Black and white hazelnut brownies

cocktail suggestion
Classic Dingle Gin Tonic (page 252)

beverage suggestion
Porterhouse Red Ale, Crean's Lager
or Sparkling Lemonade (page 264)

BBQ CHICKEN WINGS

Serves 6

24 chicken wings, whole, tip segment cut off and saved for stock

1 tsp sea salt

½ tsp garlic powder

½ tsp caster (superfine) sugar

½ tsp paprika

½ tsp ground black pepper

2 tbsp oil, for greasing

For the sauce:

120ml / 4fl oz / ½ cup ketchup

60ml / 2fl oz / ¼ cup honey

30g / 1oz / 2 tbsp butter

1 small red chilli, ribbed, seeded and finely chopped

1 tbsp Lea & Perrins Worcestershire sauce

1 tbsp smoked paprika

Preheat the oven to 170°C / 340°F / gas mark 3. Wash and pat dry the chicken wings.

Mix dry seasonings together in a small bowl, place wings into a large bowl and season with all but a half teaspoon of the seasoning blend. Save that for after the wings are sauced. Oil a baking tray and spread wings evenly in a single layer. Roast for 30 minutes.

While the wings are roasting, place all the sauce ingredients in a saucepan and simmer over low heat, stirring occasionally so that it does not stick to the bottom and burn.

When wings are cooked, place them in a large mixing bowl and pour hot BBQ sauce over them. Toss to coat. Arrange on a serving platter and sprinkle with reserved spice mix.

Chef's tip:
30g / 1oz / 2 tbsp of your favourite hot pepper sauce will heat up the sauce if you like.

MEATBALLS IN TOMATO AND MUSHROOM FONDUE

Makes approx. 30 meatballs

For the meatballs:

500g / 1lb 2oz lean minced (ground) beef

250g / 9oz minced (ground) pork

3 tbsp olive oil

1 small onion, finely chopped

3 garlic cloves, finely chopped

½ bunch (about ¼ cup) finely chopped fresh parsley

125g / 4½oz / 1 cup fresh breadcrumbs

150ml / 5¼fl oz / ⅔ cup milk

2 egg whites

salt and freshly ground black pepper

oil, for greasing

For the sauce:

1 small punnet (basket) – about 150g / 5¼oz – small button mushrooms

1 small onion, finely chopped

30g / 1oz / 2 tbsp butter

2 tbsp olive oil

2 garlic cloves, finely chopped

1 tbsp dried marjoram

60ml / 2fl oz / ¼ cup white wine

1 litre / 1¾ pints / 4 cups tomato passata (tomato sauce, to my US readers)

Chef's tip: 2 slices of white pan (sandwich bread), crust removed and torn into pieces, can replace breadcrumbs.

Preheat the oven to 160°C / 320°F / gas mark 3.

In a large mixing bowl, combine beef and pork – do not overmix.

Heat a small sauté pan over medium high heat. Add oil and onion, stirring until soft – about 5 minutes. Add the finely chopped garlic and stir for about 30 seconds, until fragrant. Remove from heat, add parsley and cool slightly.

Place breadcrumbs in a bowl and stir in milk.

Mix egg whites, onion mixture, breadcrumbs/milk, salt and pepper into the meat until well combined, being careful not to overmix.

Divide into 30 portions – about 25g / ¾–1oz each – and roll into balls. Can be made larger or smaller as you like (simply adjust the cooking time) and place on an oiled baking tray in a single layer. Roast for 20 minutes, until they reach 68°C / 155°F.

To make the sauce, place mushrooms, onion, butter and oil in a medium saucepan. Place over medium heat and cook, covered, for about 10 minutes, until mushrooms have softened a little and have given off some of their liquid.

Add garlic and cook, uncovered, until most of the liquid has evaporated. Do not let brown.

Add marjoram and stir to combine. Add white wine and let reduce by about one third. Add tomato passata and simmer while meatballs are cooking.

Stir cooked meatballs into tomato/mushroom sauce and serve with cocktail forks.

BAKED SWEET POTATO WEDGES

Serves 6

4 medium sweet potatoes
60ml / 2fl oz / ¼ cup olive oil
1 garlic clove, crushed
1 tbsp sea salt
1 tsp ground black pepper
2 tsp smoked paprika

Preheat the oven to 170°C / 340°F / gas mark 3.

Cut sweet potatoes lengthwise into eight wedges. Place in a large bowl with cold water for 15 minutes. This will help leach out some of the starch in the sweet potatoes and the bit of water they absorb will help them to cook more quickly and evenly.

Combine oil, garlic, salt, pepper and paprika in a small saucepan and warm over low heat, then drain the potatoes and pat dry. Place in a large mixing bowl and toss with oil/spice mixture, making sure to get the spices evenly distributed on the wedges.

Line a baking tray with non-stick baking paper and lay the wedges evenly on one side (not on the skin side).

Bake for 20 minutes, turn the wedges over on their other side and continue to bake for a further 10 minutes.

Chef's tip:
Jean-Marie's aioli
(page 94) is a fun
dipping sauce for
these wedges.

HOMEMADE PIZZA

Makes 1 large pizza

300g / 10½oz / 2 cups strong white flour (bread flour)

300g / 10½oz / 2 cups plain (all-purpose) flour

2 tbsp fresh yeast or 1½ sachets dried (not instant) yeast

1 tbsp sugar

2 tsp sea salt

200ml / 7fl oz / ¾ cup + 4 tsp lukewarm water

2 tbsp olive oil

Chef's tip:
Golden caster sugar is also known as turbinado or raw sugar. It is made from the first pressing of sugar cane and its crystals are a bit larger than granulated sugar. It's light brown in colour with a pleasant, light caramel flavour.

For the sauce:

225g / 8oz tomato passata (tomato sauce, to my US readers)

3 tbsp tomato purée (paste)

2 tbsp chopped fresh basil

1 tbsp turbinado sugar

2 tsp dried marjoram

Toppings:

110g / 4oz chorizo or pepperoni, sliced thin

110g / 4oz cooked ham, cut into small dice

Half a 560g / 19½oz can of pineapple, drained and roughly chopped

170g / 6oz Toonsbridge or other good-quality fresh mozzarella cheese, sliced

Preheat the oven to 200°C / 400°F / gas mark 6.

Mix flours, yeast, sugar and salt in a large bowl. Stir in water gradually to form a dough. Turn out onto lightly floured surface and knead until a smooth ball is formed (about 5 minutes).

Pour 1 tablespoon of oil into a large bowl and rub all over. Place dough in bowl – turning to coat in oil – cover with a clean tea towel and let rest in warm place to rise for 30–50 minutes, until nearly doubled in size.

Whisk all sauce ingredients together in a small bowl. Assemble topping ingredients.

Use the other tablespoon of oil to grease a baking tray. Press the risen dough into the tray (either in a circle or a rectangle to fit the baking tray), leaving a thicker edge that can be turned up to form a crust. (For crisp dough, place dough tray into oven and immediately reduce heat to 180°C / 350°F / gas mark 4. Bake for 15 minutes before removing and topping.)

Top pizza with 370ml / 13fl oz / 1½ cups of tomato pizza sauce, scatter chorizo, ham and pineapple over sauce and top with shredded cheese.

Bake for an additional 8–10 minutes, until cheese is melted. Allow to cool for 2 minutes before cutting.

BLACK AND WHITE HAZELNUT BROWNIES

Makes 6–8

180g / 6¼oz / ¾ cup butter, plus extra for greasing

300g / 10½oz / 1½ cups sugar

150g / 5¼oz / 1 cup self-raising flour

1 tsp vanilla extract

3 large eggs, beaten

75g / 2½oz dark chocolate, chopped

100g / 3½oz / ⅔ cup hazelnuts, toasted and chopped

1 tbsp cocoa powder

75g / 2½oz white chocolate, chopped

vanilla ice cream, to serve

Preheat the oven to 170°C / 340°F / gas mark 3. Grease a 20cm x 15cm / 8in x 6in baking tray.

In a medium saucepan, melt butter and sugar over low heat, stirring so it does not burn. Stir in flour and vanilla. Remove from heat and cool for a few minutes, then stir in eggs.

Divide batter between two bowls. Into one bowl add dark chocolate, hazelnuts and cocoa powder, stir to melt and blend. Into the other bowl add white chocolate and stir to melt and blend.

Place alternating spoonfuls of white and dark batter onto the greased baking tray. Swirl together with a small sharp knife.

Bake for 35 minutes and allow to cool for 10 minutes before cutting. Serve with vanilla ice cream.

Chef's tip:
Self-raising flour can be made if you don't have it on hand: 150g / 5¼oz / 1 cup plain (all-purpose) flour, 1½ tsp baking powder, ½ tsp table salt - sifted together twice and then measured as needed.

FROM A WILD AND BEAUTIFUL PLACE

*Keep an eye out for John Moriarty cycling in his high-vis
gear the next time you drive around Slea Head*

BORN ABOUT THREE MILES north-west of Dingle town in Ballycaneeen Glens, John Moriarty, one of nine children, grew up on the family farm just like three generations of children did before him. His childhood was steeped in west Kerry tradition, Irish language and Dingle sensibility. John has raised his family on the land of that same farm and his son now runs that business. Though he travelled to the continent for a year's work experience, as was all but required of Irish chefs who wanted to be taken seriously back in the day (and even to an extent to this day), he is a Dingle man through and through.

John and I sat in wing-backed chairs in front of an open fire in his restaurant as he told me stories of his family, of his cooking and of how he and Dingle's food scene grew up together over the past sixty years.

Only the second person from the peninsula to be professionally trained as a chef, John had to be convinced by his mother to accept a scholarship to the Rockwell Catering College in Tipperary. A west Kerry boy for ever, he returned to the newly opened Dingle Skellig Hotel as a commis chef in the latter half of the 1960s.

Many will know this time in Dingle history as the *Ryan's Daughter* years. David Lean brought Hollywood to the peninsula for an extensive filming period. In fact, the hotel was booked for two years, keeping the town and the hotel staff jumping with work. With hardly a restaurant in Dingle at the time, hotels and the occasional guesthouse were the only places you could find a meal for ready money.

John married his wife, Maureen, whose family was one of the last to leave the Blasket Islands, and took on the challenge of opening the Hillgrove Hotel, where he was hired to be their first head chef.

After eighteen years of catering many of the weddings and family events of Dingle, raising their own family of four children and finding the perfect location in the form of Dingle's oldest licensed premises, the time was ripe to open his own restaurant. Just like the first time he was allowed to take the horse cart into the town dairy with the tank of milk at the age of twelve or thirteen, he was on his own in a world he'd been preparing to be in for years.

The past meets the present for many families here in Dingle. John's grandchildren are being educated at the same school his grandfather attended in his schooldays. It's not uncommon to see three generations of local or visiting families dining on John's culinary offerings at Lord Baker's Restaurant, where one of his sons works as a manager and his son-in-law does most of the cooking these days.

To this day, when family gather at the Moriarty farm, they regale the young ones with stories of haymaking and milking and that old grey horse who would stop at the chemist's shop and begin to go back home if you didn't catch her in time. The memories of the times and places of the past are never far from the present with John and his family. John brings wholesome local foods from the Moriarty family farm and its surrounds to the table when his family gather on the farm in what David Lean called 'a wild and beautiful place'.

A duck dinner may sound like a 'holiday only' affair, but with a little planning, this meal can be a special weekend supper. John's menu harks back to an earlier time with favourite family recipes that have been and will be passed down from one Moriarty generation to the next. Mark Murphy's potato and turnip gratin (page 121) would also make a nice side for this menu.

A FARMHOUSE SUNDAY LUNCH

starter
Classic Dingle Bay prawn cocktail with Marie Rose sauce

main
Slow-roasted duck with blood orange sauce

sides
Apricot stuffing
Stir-fried vegetables
Duck-fat roast potatoes

dessert
Eton mess

cocktail suggestion
Cucumber Collins (page 253)

wine suggestion
New Zealand Pinot Noir

CLASSIC DINGLE BAY PRAWN COCKTAIL WITH MARIE ROSE SAUCE

Serves 6

600g / 1lb 5oz Dingle Bay prawn tails

2 tbsp sea salt

2 tsp ground black pepper

½ lemon

2 heads of butterhead lettuce

4 plum tomatoes, quartered, seeded and diced

lemon wedges, to garnish

chopped fresh parsley, to garnish

For the sauce:

300ml / ½ pint / 1¼ cups mayonnaise

salt and freshly ground black pepper

½ lemon, juiced

3 dashes of Tabasco sauce

120ml / 4fl oz / ½ cup dry sherry

2 tbsp tomato ketchup

1 tbsp tomato purée (paste)

1 tsp brandy

Place prawn tails in a saucepan with 1 litre / 1¾ pints / 4 cups of cold water with salt and pepper. Bring to a simmer and poach for 2 minutes, until just done. Drain, lay out on a cold tray in a single layer and squeeze lemon juice over the tails. Allow to cool completely.

To make the sauce, mix the mayonnaise with salt and pepper to taste in a small bowl. Stir in juice of ½ lemon, Tabasco sauce and sherry. Whisk until blended.

In a small bowl, mix ketchup, tomato purée and brandy until smooth. Blend tomato mixture into mayonnaise mixture. Chill.

Remove six leaves from the lettuce to use as cups. Wash, dry and roughly chop the remaining lettuce.

Place lettuce cups onto plates or in serving glasses. Add chopped lettuce, tomato and chilled prawns.

Spoon 1–2 tablespoons of the sauce over prawns. Dip lemon wedges into chopped parsley and use as a garnish.

Chef's tip: Large, wild shrimps can be used in place of prawns if prawns are hard to come by

SLOW-ROASTED DUCK WITH BLOOD ORANGE SAUCE

Serves 6

3 ducks, cut in half
3 tbsp coarse sea salt
8 blood oranges, zest and juice (reserve the squeezed halves)
12 sprigs fresh thyme
100g / 3½oz / ½ cup dark brown sugar
2 tbsp rice wine vinegar
750ml / 1¼ pints / 3 cups rich duck or chicken stock (to augment duck roasting liquid)

Preheat the oven to 180°C / 350°F / gas mark 4.

Rub duck halves all over with squeezed orange halves, then rub salt and 1 teaspoon of the zest into the skin and underside of each duck half. Quarter spent oranges. Place each duck half, skin side up, on wire racks set over deep baking trays. Place four squeezed orange quarters and two sprigs of thyme under each duck half.

Put into the oven and immediately turn the temperature down to 170°C / 340°F / gas mark 3. Roast for 1 hour and 45 minutes, turning and rotating pans (front to back and top to bottom) at about the halfway point.

Allow ducks to rest, tented with foil, while you make the sauce. Strain drippings, skim off the fat and set aside.

To make the sauce, heat brown sugar and vinegar in sauce pan until caramelised and thick. Add orange juice, defatted drippings plus enough stock to make 1 litre / 1¾ pints / 4 cups, simmer and reduce until it reaches desired thickness. Strain and add orange zest. Reserve 60ml / 2fl oz / ¼ cup of sauce for vegetables.

Chef's tip:
Blood oranges can be substituted but try to use oranges that are more acidic than sweet so the sauce isn't cloying and balances the rich duck

APRICOT STUFFING

Serves 6

225g / 8oz / 1 cup butter

1 large white onion, medium diced

1 tsp salt

90g / 3oz fresh apricots, stoned and chopped coarsely (dried work too, but soak for 10 minutes in warm water before using)

1 tsp chopped fresh thyme

1 tsp chopped fresh basil

1 tsp chopped fresh marjoram

120ml / 4fl oz / ½ cup sherry

360g / 12½oz / 3 cups fresh breadcrumbs

45g / 1½oz / 3 tbsp butter, for greasing

salt and freshly ground black pepper

Preheat the oven to 170°C / 340°F / gas mark 3.

Melt butter in large sauté pan over medium heat, add onion and 1 teaspoon of salt. Cook until translucent. Add apricots and herbs. Sweat for another 5 minutes. Add sherry, deglaze and simmer until almost dry. Add crumbs and mix thoroughly. Season to taste.

Butter a large baking dish. Add stuffing and bake alongside ducks at 170°C / 340°F / gas mark 3 for the last 45 minutes that they are in the oven.

STIR-FRIED VEGETABLES

Serves 6

2–3 tbsp good-quality Irish rapeseed oil

1 white onion, sliced top to bottom (French sliced)

1 red pepper, seeded and sliced top to bottom

1 green bell pepper, seeded and sliced top to bottom

1 red onion, sliced top to bottom (French sliced)

½ head of red cabbage, cored and thinly shredded

3 courgettes (zucchini), sliced into thick coins

60ml / 2fl oz / ¼ cup blood orange sauce from ducks

Preheat a large sauté pan or wok over high heat. Add oil and heat until shimmering but not smoking.

Add all vegetables except the courgettes. Stir-fry for 2 minutes. Add courgettes and stir-fry until done to your liking. Toss in the reserved blood orange sauce.

DUCK-FAT ROAST POTATOES

Serves 6

15 small or medium Rooster potatoes
200ml / 7fl oz / ¾ cup + 4 tsp duck fat
salt and freshly ground black pepper

Preheat the oven to 200°C / 400°F / gas mark 6. Place a baking tray in the oven to heat up. Wash and peel potatoes, cut in half lengthwise. Place in a large pot of salted cold water over medium–high heat. Bring to a simmer and remove from heat. Drain parboiled potatoes and lay out to dry.

Melt duck fat and toss with potatoes. Season with salt and pepper.

Spread over preheated baking tray. Place in hot oven and reduce temperature to 180°C / 350°F / gas mark 4. Roast for 25–35 minutes (depending on size), shaking and tossing two or three times, until done inside and golden brown and crisp outside.

ETON MESS

Serves 6

6 large egg whites
120g / 4¼oz / ⅔ cup caster (superfine) sugar
2 punnets (baskets) of strawberries, washed, hulled and roughly chopped
2 tbsp icing (powdered) sugar
800ml / 28fl oz / 3¼ cups double (heavy) cream

Preheat the oven to 145°C / 290°F / gas mark 2. Place a silicone baking liner on a baking tray. Put egg whites into a clean, cold bowl and whip to soft peaks. Add sugar by the spoonful and continue to whip until all sugar is incorporated and whites are firmer.

Scoop large spoonfuls of mixture onto baking tray. Place in oven and immediately turn down to 120°C / 250°F / gas mark ½. Do not open oven. After 1 hour 15 minutes, turn oven off and leave meringues in oven overnight to dry out.

Place one quarter of the chopped strawberries into a blender with the icing sugar. Purée and pass through a fine-mesh sieve.

To assemble: whip the cream to firm peaks.

Break meringues into a mixing bowl and add the strawberries. Fold in the whipped cream to distribute meringue and berries. Drizzle purée over and fold in, leaving streaks of purée throughout the dessert.

Serve in a large glass bowl to be dished out at the table.

STELLA DOYLE

Doyle's (founder)

LIVING THE GOOD LIFE

With a pan or a brush, Stella is a true artist

Brainse Rinn Na Seád
Ringsend Branch   Tel: 6680063

AS A YOUNG CHILD IN DUBLIN, Stella Doyle played at mock battles in support of the High King Brian Boru on the grounds of the ruined Clontarf Castle. She may also have been emulating her father, who joined the Volunteers after the 1916 Easter Rising and made a career as an officer in the Irish army.

Stella's mother – 'Mummy' to her and her sister – was a very good cook but wouldn't suffer her daughters in the kitchen, so there was no learning at the apron strings for these two Dublin girls.

Sitting at her substantial kitchen table, we shared a cup of tea and talked about Stella's food epiphany at a convent school in France in the early 1960s after she'd been dropped from the rolls of the College of Art with a letter to her parents stating that she was 'just not good enough' for studies in the fine arts. It was the artistic bent in her work that would eventually bring Stella to her post as owner and chef of one of Dingle's first restaurants, Doyle's.

While teaching English at the convent in the countryside near Dijon, Stella would sit in on classes with the girls to learn the French language. More important, she also learned about French food.

The farmers' daughters who attended the convent school must have thought it odd that this young Irish woman was fawning over school foods they wouldn't give to a pig. They began inviting her to their homes at the weekends, where the mothers would cook Sunday lunches of game, frogs' legs and dairy produce. The lavish dishes were, for the most part, made with ingredients available in Ireland, but oh, they were cooked so differently.

At twenty-four, Stella married an advertising agency director who was wrung out from that stressful career. Two years later, Stella and John came to Dingle, where they bought a boat, intending to 'live the good life' as a commercial fisherman and his shore-hand wife in the newly established crab fishery.

During a year or so of the hard labour that is fishing, Stella noted that tourists watching the fresh crab, lobster and finfish being offloaded at the pier were asking where they could get the day's catch served to them for dinner. Back then, most of it was going to France and Spain. Cue a bright flash of the obvious: someone should open a restaurant serving Dingle seafood! Thus, Doyle's opened in 1972.

Not having any experience in the business, Stella spent some weeks standing in the corners and along the kitchen walls of Arbutus Lodge in Cork (which would go on to win a Michelin star), wide-eyed and taking pages of notes.

Stella's memory of the early days of Dingle food is encyclopaedic. She remembers the names of the shopkeepers and farmers, the fishermen and their wives. Stories of which fisherman's wife made the best crab pâté, who would order in a speciality ingredient for her and who might forage for the best local oysters flow as easy as milk into our second cuppa.

Until she sold Doyle's in 1998, the tastes of Dingle locals and tourists were shaped by Stella's deft hand in the kitchen and John's taste in the wines of the world. As her sense of cooking local ingredients evolved, so, too, did the tastes of the peninsula.

In her book *1,000 Places to See Before You Die*, Patricia Schultz listed 'eat at Doyle's' in the first 100 pages. From failed art student falling in love with French convent food to trailblazing west Kerry restaurateur, it can certainly be said that Stella has indeed lived the good life that she and John sought here so many years ago.

Like many of the chefs I interviewed for this book, Stella uses in her menu some of the recipes from her days in the restaurant that she might eat as her own quick supper on a busy night. You'll want to have her mackerel pâté in the refrigerator at all times for a quick snack or a light lunch. It also goes well with Lee Sim's pan de aceite (page 246).

A FINE SUMMER EVENING

starter
Smoked mackerel pâté in cherry tomatoes with salsa verde

main
Pasta with Dingle Bay prawns in white wine and saffron sauce

side
Mixed greens salad with Billy's French dressing

dessert
Mum's sponge cake with berries and cream

cocktail suggestion
Prosecco Cocktail (page 261)

wine suggestion
Tavel rosé

SMOKED MACKEREL PÂTÉ IN CHERRY TOMATOES WITH SALSA VERDE

Serves 6

2 whole smoked mackerel (or 4 fillets)

1 x 225g / 8oz tub of cottage cheese

freshly ground black pepper

2 tbsp lemon juice

2 punnets (baskets) of ripe cherry tomatoes

lemon wedges, to garnish

rocket (arugula), to garnish

For the salsa verde:

25g / ¾oz / 1 cup fresh parsley

1 garlic clove

80ml / 3fl oz / ⅓ cup olive oil

1 tbsp white wine vinegar

1 tsp capers

1 anchovy

Skin the mackerel and carefully take off the bone, making sure there are no small bones. Put into a food processor with the cottage cheese, plenty of pepper and add lemon juice to taste. Pulse until well blended and smooth. Fill piping bag with star tip with the pâté.

Slice the tops from tomatoes and scoop out the seeds. Take a thin slice off the bottom of each so they sit flat. Pipe the pâté into the tomatoes.

To make the salsa verde, place all ingredients into a blender and blend until smooth, scraping down as needed.

Dot each plate with about 2 tablespoons of sauce and arrange the filled tomatoes on top. Garnish with lemon wedges and rocket.

Chef's tip:
Not a fan of mackerel? Try smoked trout or hot-smoked salmon (not cold-smoked or gravlax) or even smoked tuna. Just cut the lemon juice down a bit as these other fish won't require quite as much.

PASTA WITH DINGLE BAY PRAWNS IN WHITE WINE AND SAFFRON SAUCE

Serves 6

600g / 1lb 5oz linguine
200ml / 7fl oz / ¾ cup + 4 tsp white wine
pinch of saffron
75g / 2½oz / 5 tbsp butter
600g / 1lb 5oz Dingle Bay prawns
2 garlic cloves, crushed
60ml / 2fl oz / ¼ cup cream (optional)
squeeze of lemon juice
salt and freshly ground black pepper
2 tbsp chopped fresh parsley

Cook the pasta in a large pot of boiling water until al dente.

Steep saffron in white wine.

Heat a knob of butter in a large pan, let sizzle, add prawns and fry until they change colour, 1–2 minutes. Take prawns out and set aside.

Add the garlic, sizzle but do not brown – about 30 seconds. Add the wine with saffron, bring to the boil and let reduce by half. Add the rest of the butter and cream, if using, a squeeze of lemon, salt and pepper to taste. Add back the prawns and reheat, add the parsley, toss into the pasta.

MIXED GREENS SALAD WITH BILLY'S FRENCH DRESSING

Serves 6

300g / 10½oz hearty mixed salad greens, including escarole, radicchio, leaf and baby chard if possible

For the dressing:

150ml / 5¼fl oz / ⅔ cup olive oil

60ml / 2fl oz / ¼ cup white wine vinegar

1 garlic clove

1 spring onion (scallion)

2 sprigs of fresh parsley

1 tsp Dijon mustard

salt and freshly ground black pepper

Wash and dry salad greens, then place in a large mixing bowl.

Place all dressing ingredients in a blender and mix until emulsified. Dress salad as you like, toss and serve.

MUM'S SPONGE CAKE WITH BERRIES AND CREAM

Serves 6–8

3 eggs

85g / 3oz / ⅓ cup + 2 tbsp caster (superfine) sugar

85g / 3oz / ¾ cup plain (all-purpose) flour, sifted

450g / 1lb strawberries, cleaned, hulled and halved (or mixed berries)

250ml / 9fl oz / 1 cup cream, stiffly whipped

icing (powdered) sugar, to decorate

whole fresh berries, to decorate

sprig of fresh mint, to decorate

Preheat the oven to 180°C / 350°F / gas mark 4.

Put eggs and sugar in a mixer and whisk to ribbon stage. Fold in flour and pour into two lined and greased 18cm / 7in cake tins. Bake for 35 minutes. Let cool completely before taking out of tin.

Spread cream on top of one layer, arrange berries on top of cream and place the second sponge on top of that. Dust with icing sugar and decorate with whole fresh berries and a sprig of fresh mint.

PAT MOORE

Beginish

IN THE MAIL ROAD

With Lyric FM on the radio and a deck in her hand,
Pat's favourite room in the house is still the kitchen

BY THE TIME MANY CHEFS are in their mid-fifties, they are beginning to look at ways to get out of the kitchen. But Pat Moore is not like many of the chefs I've met. In fact, she's not like many *people* I've ever met. She opened Beginish on Green Street in Dingle when she was fifty-four and had no more professional cooking experience than a six-week course at La Varenne in Paris.

Pat met her husband, John, when they both worked in the airline industry at Shannon Airport in the 1950s. While the couple were getting ready to emigrate to Canada for career advancement in the field, John's parents, who owned the local cinema at the time, encouraged them to move to Dingle instead. They did, making Pat someone known as coming 'in the Mail Road' at the time. Today the locals use the term 'blow-in' for those of us who have made our way to Dingle from other parts of Ireland and the world.

Proving herself to be a formidable woman indeed, Pat decided to buy a substantial house in the town, which was reputed to be haunted, and turn it into a guesthouse, Beginish House, named for the smallest of the Blasket Islands. (The Irish *beiginis* translates as 'small island'.)

While raising their four children, Pat ran the guesthouse and opened first one, then a second Irish crafts shop in Dingle, which they ran into the 1980s. Then, for another challenge, she opened a tearoom in another property, which she thought her daughter might run when she came home from university in Paris.

This was not to be, though, as said daughter had met and fallen in love with the Frenchman she would eventually marry. However, she did come to visit her mother and suggested that she change the tearoom into a proper restaurant, and so she did.

The restaurant (also called Beginish) was an immediate success, with John serving as host and Pat running the newly remodelled kitchen. She developed close relations with local purveyors and took *stages* with the likes of Agnes Amberg, Zurich's highest-acclaimed chef of the era, expanding the reputation of both Beginish and the whole of Dingle. For the nearly twenty years that her restaurant was open, it was not uncommon for people visiting the country to make a special trip to the peninsula just to eat Pat Moore's food between St Patrick's Day and the first of November, the only months Dingle drew tourists back in the day.

Pat's father was an academic with diverse tastes in literature, music, archaeology and art and her mother was the only child of a Cork business family, so Pat seems to have inherited a brilliant mix of shrewd business acumen and an artistic sensibility, spiced with a lust for knowledge. The cookbooks stuffed onto a kitchen shelf next to her beloved Aga range from *Larousse Gastronomique* to a popular Chinese guide from the 1970s to Irma Rombauer's *Joy of Cooking*. Eclectic, to be sure, but telling of Pat's passion for learning and doing.

Not only did she bring Irish classics with a French twist to Dingle, but Pat also introduced elegant silverware from the continent, like saucier spoons, as well as recipes from America that her children would bring back from their J1 visa stints.

Though she and her family travelled extensively, every lovely place they visited was typically compared to – and always lost out to – their home of Dingle. Pat's passion for the beauty of the place and the people who welcomed her when she and John moved here in 1965 is still obvious when she speaks of them. She told me that she 'landed on her feet' when she spoke of falling in love with a Dingle man and having the right good fortune to call Dingle and Beginish home for all these years.

But all good things must end, and in 2008, at the age of seventy-five, Pat closed Beginish and sold the building but kept the name for the sake of legacy. To this day, you will hear people who love food reminiscing about Pat Moore's creations when they talk about dining in Dingle, a fitting tribute to the 'local' woman who once came 'in the Mail Road'.

A KITCHEN TABLE SUPPER

starters
Creamed cauliflower soup with Irish blue cheese

main
Pat's fish pie

dessert
Whiskey and sherry trifle

cocktail suggestion
Cranberry Fishbowl (page 253)

wine suggestion
Vinho Verde

With the exception of her role as her family's official trifle maker, Pat doesn't do much in the way of entertaining any more. Her husband teased her for offering up a fish pie supper as her menu, but I'm glad she did. The best ingredients and a simple hand make this menu high on my list for rainy afternoon cookery. Add in Anne Long's baby gem salad (page 132) and you've got the perfect sideboard buffet.

CREAMED CAULIFLOWER SOUP WITH IRISH BLUE CHEESE

Serves 6

1 onion

1 head of cauliflower

3 small potatoes, washed and peeled

3 stalks celery, washed and ribbed

60g / 2oz / 4 tbsp butter

2 garlic cloves, sliced

1 litre / 1¾ pints / 4 cups chicken stock

200ml / 7fl oz / ¾ cup + 4 tsp cream

100g / 3½oz / ¾ cup crumbled Crozier or Cashel Blue (or any mild Irish blue cheese of your liking)

salt and freshly ground black pepper

Chop all the vegetables into pieces about 1cm / ½in big.

Melt butter in a heavy-bottomed pot over medium–low heat and add onion. Cook until soft. Add garlic and stir for 30 seconds. Add all other vegetables and cook, stirring often so they do not brown, until they begin to soften – about 8 minutes.

Add stock (plus water to cover if needed) and bring to a simmer. Cook until all vegetables are soft – about 25 minutes.

Purée soup in two batches in a blender or using a hand-held blender until very smooth. Stir in the cream and cheese, season to taste and serve.

Chef's tip:
Use floury potatoes - like a Queen, Kerr's Pink or Russet - for this dish. The starch in the potato will help thicken the soup nicely and give it an added dimension of flavour.

PAT'S FISH PIE

Serves 6

1kg / 2¼lb mixed fish, such as cod, hake, salmon, monk and/or haddock (go very light on any smoked fish you use as you don't want it to overwhelm the dish)

5–6 king prawns per person (30–36 total)

950ml / 33fl oz / 3¾ cups milk

½ onion

1 bay leaf

2 cloves

6 peppercorns

100g / 3½oz / ½ cup butter

2 shallots, finely chopped

50g / 1¾oz / ⅔ cup plain flour

100g / 3½oz baby spinach

900g / 2lb mashed potatoes

salt and pepper

Chef's tip:
Many fishmongers will have a mixture of fish for chowders and pies already cut and mixed. I prefer to buy small amounts of the freshest fish of the day and cut my own. It's an extra step (a very small step) but then you get the freshest fish and can choose what you like.

Preheat the oven to 180°C / 350°F / gas mark 4. Cut fish and prawns into bite-sized pieces.

Place milk in a large, non-reactive pot. Spike bay leaf into onion with cloves. Add to milk with peppercorns. Bring to a simmer (do not boil).

Add fish to simmering milk and gently poach for 2 minutes. Remove fish and put it on a large cold plate in one layer to cool. Continue simmering milk for 20 minutes.

Melt the butter in a saucepan, add shallots and stir for about 2 minutes. Stir in the flour and cook for an additional 2–3 minutes, stirring all the time, until pale golden.

Remove onion and peppercorns from cooking liquid. Gradually whisk the flour roux into the fish cooking liquid. Bring to a simmer until the mixture begins to thicken, then season with salt and pepper. Reduce the heat to low and allow to simmer gently for 3–4 minutes, until thickened. Take off heat and fold fish back into sauce.

Pour sauce, with the fish, into a buttered baking dish. Arrange spinach on top of fish and top with mashed potatoes (see Mike Hayes' mashed pototatoes, page 228). Bake for 15–20 minutes, until heated through and lightly browned.

WHISKEY AND SHERRY TRIFLE

Serves 6–8

For the sponge cake:

1 tbsp vegetable oil, for greasing

3 eggs

85g / 3oz / ⅓ cup + 2 tbsp caster (superfine) sugar

85g / 3oz / ¾ cup plain (all-purpose) flour

For the custard:

6 egg yolks

150g / 5¼oz / ¾ cup caster (superfine) sugar

40g / 1½oz / ¼ cup + 2 tsp plain (all-purpose) flour

pinch of salt

1.1 litres / 2 pints / 4½ cups milk

90g / 3oz / 6 tbsp unsalted butter

1 tbsp + 1 tsp vanilla extract

To assemble:

120g / 4¼oz / ½ cup raspberry or other fruit jam (I love gooseberry jam in my trifle!)

60ml / 2fl oz / ¼ cup simple syrup (2 tbsp sugar and 2 tbsp water brought to a boil and cooled)

60ml / 2fl oz / ¼ cup sherry cask-aged Dingle whiskey

60ml / 2fl oz / ¼ cup dry sherry

250ml / 9fl oz / 1 cup cream, whipped

fresh berries, to decorate (if you can, match the fruit to the jam)

Preheat the oven to 180°C / 350°F / gas mark 4. Grease two 25cm x 33cm (9in x 13in) baking trays with half the tablespoon of vegetable oil each.

To make the sponge, whip the eggs and sugar until they reach the ribbon stage. Sift flour over egg mixture and gently fold together. Divide batter into greased baking tins. Bake for 30–40 minutes, until springy and lightly browned. Cool completely before using.

To make the custard, beat yolks and sugar in a medium bowl until well mixed. Sift flour and salt together. Stir into eggs. Add 60ml / 2fl oz / ¼ cup of milk and mix well.

In a small saucepan, heat remaining milk and butter over medium heat until butter is melted and mixture begins to steam – do not boil. Remove from heat and add to egg mixture 60ml / 2fl oz / ¼ cup at a time, stirring the eggs very well so they do not scramble.

Place mixture in saucepan and return to heat, stirring constantly. Cook until the custard reaches 70°C / 160°F and has thickened.

Remove from heat and pass through a fine-mesh sieve into a clean bowl. Stir in vanilla. Use while still warm and pourable.

To assemble, cut sponge into 5cm x 8cm / 2in x 3in rectangles and prick with a fork. Spread sponge pieces with jam and sandwich together. Set aside.

Add whiskey and sherry to syrup.

Place one quarter of the sponge pieces into a glass bowl. Sprinkle with one quarter of the fortified syrup. Pour one quarter of the custard onto cake. Spread to cover. Repeat in layers, finishing with the final quarter of custard. Chill 4 hours or overnight.

To serve, top with whipped cream and decorate with fruit.

LAURA WALKER
Wild Banks

A MEAL TO REMEMBER

It wouldn't be a stretch to say that Laura Walker is the reason the author moved to Dingle ... Laura Walker's food, that is

MANY OF THE CHEFS IN DINGLE who migrated to this 'island on an island' came because of the chefs, restaurants and hotels you've been reading about so far. It could be said that I came to Dingle because of Laura Walker and her now-shuttered Wild Banks restaurant, which once stood on Main Street.

After travelling through Dingle on a number of occasions, I spent one night here in 2005 while touring Ireland with my brother and sister. A meal of Laura's food had me hooked. It was this taste of Dingle that whetted my appetite for a longer visit, and eventually had me shift my life from Seattle to Dingle in order to sate my hunger for more.

The Donegal native came from one land of 'bogs and rocks and mountains and lakes ... and rain', as she put it, to another. But in true 'Forgotten County' form, she says that Donegal is nicer. Even the wonders of 'the Kingdom' can't wash away the fond memories she has of her childhood in the tidy coastal town of Glenties.

Her mother was certified as a chef and worked in the Great Northern Hotel as well as her uncle's inn outside their town. She gave up the station behind the stove when she married, however, to raise her six children, of whom Laura is the second eldest of four girls and two boys. She inherited her mother's passion and talent for cooking and knew from a young age that cooking was the profession for her.

After studying for her certification, Laura worked in and around Galway and Cork before landing a second-chef job at a new restaurant in Cork city. After two years in Cork, she did her time on the continent for 24 months in the Black Forest region of Germany at fine hotels, which she thoroughly enjoyed, but home was calling.

'Home', as it were, came in the form of a call from the owner of the new Charthouse Restaurant here in Dingle. During the next couple of busy years she met a man called Paul Walker, but she was soon back working in Cork in a friend's new restaurant.

Love being what it is and Dingle being Dingle, she packed up and left the Rebel County to come back for Paul and a new gig running the food service for the Dingle links golf club at Ceann Sibéal – a long, long time before the area became known for its location as the Jedi training camp in the *Star Wars* franchise.

This time – the time in between Ceann Sibéal and the birth of her children, Liam and Clíodhna – was when Laura poured her cooking heart and foodie soul into her own restaurant, the Wild Banks.

Dingle in the 1990s was a booming place, but it was difficult for a new restaurant to get a foothold with culinary pillars like Doyle's, the Beginish, Lord Baker's and the Half Door all just a few steps from her door. With food that pushed tradition in the days before customers were ready to bend and given increasing rent and expenses, a nationwide chef shortage and their first child on the way, Laura decided to step back from the long days of being a chef and into the even longer days (and nights) of being a mother.

I'll never forget my first – and only – meal at the Wild Banks. I don't remember what I ate that evening, but I do remember that it was wonderful and that it really was the reason I considered moving to Dingle. It's hard for me to believe that that will be the only meal to be cooked for me by this formidable culinary talent, but at least we can all savour the menu she has proffered. It's a glimpse into a brief moment in Dingle culinary history that we hope to see resurrected.

Using ingredients that many people will have in the larder or refrigerator already, Laura has put together a menu that could be thrown together at short notice. Swap the pickled cabbage with Denis O'Connor's roasted asparagus (page 66) and the meal goes from autumn/winter to spring/summer in a flash. And after tasting this chilli ice cream, you'll want to have a container in the freezer at all times. I know I do.

FRIDAY NIGHT BACK WEST

starter
Seared scallops with chilli jam

main
Roast pork fillet with apricot and raisin stuffing and balsamic cream

sides
Garlic crushed potatoes
Pickled red cabbage

dessert
Tempura fried strawberries with chilli ice cream

cocktail suggestion
Bramble (page 252)

wine suggestion
Alsatian Riesling or Pinot Gris

SEARED SCALLOPS WITH CHILLI JAM

Serves 6

For the chilli jam:

12 red chillies, roughly chopped with seeds (cayenne or Kung Pao work well)
1 red bell pepper, roughly chopped with seeds
450g / 1lb jam sugar
1 litre / 1¾ pints / 4 cups red wine vinegar
600ml / 1 pint / 2⅓ cups water
200ml / 7fl oz / ¾ cup + 4 tsp (approx.) apple juice

18 medium scallops
60g / 2oz / 4 tbsp butter
4 tbsp olive oil
salt and freshly ground black pepper

100g / 3½oz rocket (arugula)
½ lemon, juiced

Place chillies, bell pepper, sugar, vinegar and water in a large pot. Bring to boil while stirring until sugar is dissolved. Boil steadily for about 15 minutes, until the mixture begins to look like lava.

Remove from heat and cool for 10 minutes. Pour into a blender and blend, thinning with apple juice as needed – the consistency should be like a thick sauce.

Pour into sterilised jars, cover and refrigerate. Extra jam can be used as you like.

Remove the small muscle from the scallops, rinse under cold water and pat dry. In two large, heavy-bottomed frying pans, heat 2 tablespoons of olive oil and 30g / 1oz / 2 tablespoons of butter in each until butter starts to brown. Season scallops and sear for 1–1½ minutes each side (don't overcrowd the pan). They should have a gold crust on the outside but be translucent in the centre.

Dress rocket with lemon juice and salt. Serve each plate with small salad of rocket, a dollop of chilli jam and three scallops.

Chef's tip: Don't season scallops until they are just about to go into the pan, and season lightly. The salt will draw out moisture and heavy seasoning can overpower the delicate flavour.

ROAST PORK FILLET WITH APRICOT AND RAISIN STUFFING AND BALSAMIC CREAM

Serves 6

2 x 400g / 14oz pork steaks (tenderloins)
15g / ½oz / 1 tbsp butter, softened
salt and freshly ground black pepper

For the stuffing:
100g / 3½oz / ½ cup butter
1 small onion, chopped
2 dessert apples, peeled and grated
100g / 3½oz / ⅔ cup raisins
100g / 3½oz / ½ cup dried apricots
60ml / 2fl oz / ¼ cup orange juice
200g / 7oz / 1⅔ cups fresh breadcrumbs
salt and freshly ground black pepper

For the balsamic cream:
1 tbsp olive oil
30g / 1oz / 2 tbsp butter
4 shallots, diced
1 tbsp brown sugar
2 smoked streaky rashers (bacon), chopped
1 sprig of fresh thyme
100ml / 3½fl oz / ⅓ cup + 4 tsp red wine
1 litre / 1¾ pints / 4 cups stock
1 tbsp arrowroot mixed with 2 tbsp water
100ml / 3½fl oz / ⅓ cup + 4 tsp balsamic vinegar
200ml / 7fl oz / ¾ cup + 4 tsp double (heavy) cream
salt and freshly ground black pepper

Preheat the oven to 180°C / 350°F / gas mark 4.

To make the stuffing, melt butter in a large sauté pan over medium heat. Add onion and a pinch of salt. Cook until translucent. Add fruit and orange juice, simmer till nearly dry. Add breadcrumbs and mix. Season with salt and pepper. Remove from heat and allow to cool.

To prepare the pork, remove any sinew or fat. Make a horizontal slit in each pork fillet from end to end, making sure not to cut all the way through.

Place a sheet of non-stick baking paper over each fillet and flatten with rolling pin. Season each fillet and divide the stuffing between them. Roll and tie at 8cm / 3in intervals. Spread half of the butter over the top of each. Roast in the oven for 45–60 minutes.

To make the balsamic cream, heat oil and butter in a large saucepan over medium heat. Add shallots, brown sugar and bacon, stirring often. Cook until caramelised. Add thyme, wine and stock, reduce by half, thicken with arrowroot mixture, one half at a time to desired thickness. Taste and season. Strain and set aside. This is your jus for sauce.

In a separate pan over medium–high heat, add vinegar and reduce by half, add the jus and cream, bring just to a boil and blend with hand-held blender until smooth. Correct the seasoning.

To serve, slice the pork on the bias, pour half of the sauce onto a warm serving plate and arrange pork on top of sauce. Serve remaining sauce on the side.

GARLIC CRUSHED POTATOES

Serves 6

6 tbsp olive oil
4–6 garlic cloves
1 tbsp chopped fresh rosemary
1kg / 2¼lb waxy potatoes
salt and freshly ground black pepper

In a small saucepan, heat garlic and rosemary in oil until the garlic is soft. Smash garlic with a fork. Set aside.

Starting in cold, salted water, simmer potatoes until they are just tender and drain. Crush each potato lightly (reduce height by about half) with the side of a chef's knife or the bottom of a pan. Pour over the oil and season with salt and pepper.

Chef's tip:
Waxy fingerling potatoes work nicely in this recipe as well; simply adjust the cooking time down a bit to accommodate the smaller potatoes.

PICKLED RED CABBAGE

Serves 6–8

450g / 1lb red cabbage, cored and shredded
200g / 7oz red onion, diced finely
225g / 8oz cooking apples, peeled, cored and chopped small
2 tbsp sugar
2 tbsp red wine vinegar
1 orange, zest and juice
½ tsp ground nutmeg
½ tsp ground cinnamon
¼ tsp ground cloves

DAY 1

Mix all ingredients together and place in a bowl with a smaller lid or plate on top.
Place a heavy weight – a large can of veg works well – and leave overnight.

DAY 2

Preheat the oven to 150°C / 300°F / gas mark 2.

Transfer to a casserole dish and cook, uncovered, for 1½–2 hours, until soft, stirring a
couple of times.

Chef's tip:
Tart apples, such as
Bramley, Granny Smith,
Winesap or Cox's Pippins
work very well in this
dish. If you use a sweeter
apple, consider adjusting
the amount of sugar.

TEMPURA FRIED STRAWBERRIES WITH CHILLI ICE CREAM

Serves 6

For the ice cream:

1 litre / 1¾ pints / 4 cups milk

375g / 13oz / 1¾ cups + 2 tbsp caster (superfine) sugar

5 egg yolks

500ml / 18fl oz / 2 cups cream

2 tbsp chilli jam (see page 42)

For the tempura:

85g / 3oz / ⅓ cup + 2 tbsp plain (all-purpose) flour

½ tsp salt

½ tsp caster (superfine) sugar

200ml / 7fl oz / ¾ cup + 4 tsp sparkling water, chilled

For the strawberries:

85g / 3oz / ⅓ cup + 2 tbsp plain (all-purpose) flour

2 tbsp caster (superfine) sugar

1 tbsp ground cinnamon

3 punnets (baskets) of large strawberries, hulls and stems left on

1 litre / 1¾ pints / 4 cups vegetable oil, for frying

To make the ice cream, in a heavy-bottomed pot, bring milk almost to a boil – the froth stage, just before it comes up side of the pot.

Whisk sugar and egg yolks until they have doubled in size.

Add milk into egg mixture 60ml / 2fl oz / ¼ cup at a time, stirring the eggs very well so they do not scramble. Return to a clean pot.

Simmer gently on a low heat while stirring until the mixture coats the back of a spoon. Remove from heat, transfer the mixture to a clean bowl and allow to cool to room temperature.

Stir in cream, then add the chilli jam – use more if you want the ice cream spicier. Transfer to ice cream machine, churn and freeze.

To make the tempura, lightly whisk flour, salt, sugar and sparkling water together to form light batter.

To assemble and cook the berries, place flour in a dish. Mix cinnamon and sugar together and set aside. Wash strawberries and dry well.

Heat the oil to 185°C / 365°F.

Roll 6–10 strawberries in flour at a time. Shake off excess flour. Dip into tempura batter and gently drop into oil. Fry until golden brown and crisp, about 30–60 seconds. Remove from oil and drain on kitchen paper (paper towels). Dust with the cinnamon sugar.

Repeat with the remaining strawberries (this will be a 'short order' type of dessert, as the berries are best eaten while still hot) and serve immediately with chilli ice cream.

TREVIS L. GLEASON
The Author

THE YANK ON THE BIKE

Bright copper kettles and worn, woolly Wheatens ... these are a few of his favourite things

'YOU KNOW TREVIS, THE YANK ON THE BIKE.' The number of times I've been introduced that way around Dingle makes me smile. I am indeed an American citizen, and rather than using an automobile, I get around Dingle and its environs on a rather recognisable boardwalk cruiser with white-walled tyres.

My wife and I, along with our Irish dog, Sadie, came to Dingle from Seattle in 2012, 'to live the dream while we can', as we put it. We've been welcomed by the people of Dingle far deeper and far faster than we ever had any right to hope.

My career in the food business was interrupted in 2001 by a diagnosis of multiple sclerosis. Living in Ireland had been a dream of mine since I'd first spent a winter here in 2006. That the woman who would become my wife was up for the adventure made it possible. Hope without a plan is just a dream, and she helped me make that dream come true. Like many of the chefs featured in this book, my first career had nothing to do with food. I was a ships' navigator in the US Coast Guard for nearly seven years before I succumbed to the lure of long, hot late-night hours in this profession. I studied under Michel LeBorgne at the New England Culinary Institute and worked around New England and New York before taking on a position in the School of Hotel Administration at Cornell University.

I started as a sous chef at the school's teaching hotel, the Statler, and was eventually made an instructor at the university. During my tenure, under the Clinton administration, I was honoured to be named an ambassador for the US Agency for International Development (USAID) to Ukraine, where I worked with grain farmers and entrepreneurial bakers on increasing yields and streamlining the supply chain from field to bread-buying customer. I was 30 years old at the time and am hesitant to admit that it was the first trip I'd ever taken for which I needed a passport.

My former professional colleagues scoffed at my stories of wonderful Irish food when I returned from my first winter in Dingle. Even then, the false reputation for bland, boiled Irish food lingered in America. With nearly a score of visitors returning from their trips to stay with me to validate my claims of working with some of the best produce I'd ever seen in my personal or professional life, chef friends now queue up to visit Caryn and me in Dingle to cook and dine on exquisite ingredients raised, grown, caught, shot, foraged or otherwise gathered within a 15km radius of our new home.

While my professional cooking days are far behind me, I still derive great joy from planning a meal, assembling ingredients and preparing dishes. I'm not as good at it as I once was, but at the same time, I look at my responsibility to the food differently than I did as a young chef. Back then I saw it as my job to bend food to my will, to coax creations from ingredients. Now I realise that the job of a good chef is to source impeccable ingredients and do their best not to muck them up.

It's not uncommon for any week's simple meals to include Asian, African, European, American and Latin dishes, all made with local Dingle ingredients. Like many chefs who live here, I love Irish food but thoroughly enjoy international flavours as well. Mexican chilli-braised shanks of Dingle venison with hand-rolled tortillas, Vietnamese spring rolls filled with local vegetables and duck (raised for us by a friend), Maharees cauliflower curry or a French en papillote of locally landed black sole are the types of dishes I love to cook and eat.

When our friends and family come to stay with us, however, it's 'Irish' food they desire, so it's Irish food we give them, if with a bit of a twist. The menu I offer is a typical mash-up of American and Irish flavours that we might put together for an evening of visitors and local friends meeting at our table for the first time and departing the house as old friends.

There are few things more impressive for guests at my house than entering to find a beautiful leg of Jerry Kennedy's Dingle Peninsula *pré-salé* lamb roasting in front of a glowing turf fire. With a centrepiece like that, all you need is a few sides and the star of the meal has its supporting cast. Add Maja Beaujouan's apple and avocado salad (page 103) or swap the sweet potato and mustard colcannon for Jean-Marie Vaireaux's butter-toasted quinoa (page 96) and you'll give a whole different personality to your meal.

A TASTE OF DINGLE FOR VISITORS

starter
Oysters Casino

main
Hearth-roasted leg of Dingle Peninsula lamb with foraged herb pesto

sides
Sweet potato and three-mustard colcannon

dessert
Fuchsia shortbread with Dingle gin lemon curd

cocktail suggestion
Ryan's Downfall (page 261)

wine suggestion
Cru Beaujolais such as Morgon

OYSTERS CASINO

Serves 6

3 slices of smoked streaky bacon

coarse salt, for cooking and serving

18 large local oysters

Dingle vodka

1 medium white onion, cut into 5mm / ¼in dice

1 red onion, cut into 5mm / ¼in dice

1 red bell pepper, cut into 5mm / ¼in dice

1 green bell pepper, cut into 5mm / ¼in dice

1 yellow or orange bell pepper, cut into 5mm / ¼in dice

½ jalapeño pepper, seeded, ribbed and finely chopped

hot red pepper sauce (Crystal, Franks, Tabasco, etc.)

Lea & Perrins Worcestershire sauce

170g / 6oz Beenoskee cheese (or Comté or Gruyère if young), grated

1 lemon, washed in hot water and cut into 6 wedges, to garnish

fresh coriander (cilantro), to garnish

Preheat grill (broiler) to high.

Cut bacon pieces in half, stack and cut each half into thirds, leaving 18 pieces. Place in a small saucepan, cover with cold water and bring to a boil. Drain and blot dry with kitchen paper (paper towels). Set aside.

Make three rows of coarse salt, 2.5cm / 1in deep, on a baking tray.

Shuck oysters over a bowl to catch any liquid, being very careful not to cut yourself. Discard top shell, loosen muscle from bottom shell but keep it in the shell. Place shell-side down on salted baking tray and press into salt to hold flat. Drizzle a few drops of Dingle vodka onto each oyster.

Mix both onions, all bell peppers and jalapeño in a medium-sized bowl.

Top each oyster with 1 heaped tablespoon of the pepper and onion confetti. Drizzle with reserved oyster liquid. Place 1–2 drops each of red pepper sauce and Worcestershire sauce, depending on taste, on each mound of confetti. Distribute the grated cheese evenly over the 18 oysters. Top each with one piece of the blanched bacon.

Place under the grill, about 10cm / 4in from the heat, for 3–5 minutes, until the cheese is bubbly and the bacon is sizzling.

Make a small pile of coarse salt on each plate, place three oysters on the salt. Garnish with lemon wedge and coriander.

HEARTH-ROASTED LEG OF DINGLE PENINSULA LAMB WITH FORAGED HERB PESTO

Serves 6–8

1 x 2.5kg / 5½lb leg of lamb – see note below for your butcher
500ml / 18fl oz / 2 cups high-quality Irish rapeseed oil or extra virgin olive oil
6–10 sprigs of mixed fresh herbs, tied at the base to form a 'brush'

For the pesto marinade:
200g / 7oz wild garlic or garlic chives
110g / 4oz wild nettle tops (optional but very nice)
4 garlic cloves, peeled and halved
1 bunch of fresh flat-leaf or curly parsley, bottom 1cm / ½in trimmed from stems
25g / ¾oz / 1 cup mixed fresh herbs of your choice, picked and lightly packed (reserve extra herbs for the 'brush' above)
3 tbsp flaky sea salt
1 tbsp freshly ground black pepper
250ml / 9fl oz / 1 cup high-quality Irish rapeseed oil or extra virgin olive oil

Note for your butcher: The leg should have its 'heel' intact. This is the place where the large tendon attaches to the bone. Between this tendon and the bone is where you'll pierce a hole and insert the twine for hanging. For ease of carving, also have the butcher cut out or partially cut out the aitch bone and tie it back into place with two or three butcher's knots. Ask the butcher for about 2 metres / 6½ feet of twine for hanging the leg as well.

Place wild garlic and nettles into separate small bowls. Boil a full kettle of water for each bowl. Pour boiling water over and stir for about 10 seconds. Drain and shock in ice water. Drain and spin dry.

Place blanched herbs, fresh garlic, parsley and mixed herbs of your choice in the bowl of a food processor. Pulse four or five times to break them up.

Add salt and pepper. Then, with motor running, drizzle in the oil to make a paste. Scrape down once or twice. Separate 2 tablespoons for use in basting.

Rub the remaining pesto on the leg of lamb to coat well. Wrap the leg in several layers of cling film and marinate in the refrigerator for at least 24 hours and as long as four days – the longer, the better, really.

The day of your dinner party, remove the leg of lamb at least 4 hours before cooking (and expect an additional 2–2½ hours for cooking) and let it come to room temperature, still wrapped.

About 2 hours before cooking, start a fire in the grate of your fireplace and screw a sturdy hook into the bottom of the mantle (I know, but it's worth it) from which the lamb will hang. Make sure that the leg will hang directly in front of the fire – not too close – and will have room to spin. Keep this fire well stoked to heat the whole area around the fireplace. (Note: it's best if you haven't cleaned out the grate for a fire or two so you have ashes to rake out onto the hearth to absorb any drippings.)

Using about 2 metres / 6½ feet of butcher's twine, make a loop and pass it through the hole between the leg and the tendon. Thread the two ends through the loop and pull, arranging the loop so that it encircles the joint where tendon and bone meet.

Place a small pan on the raked ashes on the hearth, under where you have screwed the hook. Suspend the leg from the hook, via the string, so that as much of the leg is exposed to direct heat as possible – usually the lower, the better. Make sure the string is tied securely to the hook.

Twist the leg for about a dozen turns in one direction and let it unwind / rewind. About every 3–5 minutes, you'll need to twist the leg again to keep it gently spinning.

In a small ovenproof pot, combine the reserved pesto with the oil and warm over medium–high heat. Remove pot to the front of the fireplace to keep warm. Place the herb 'brush' into the oil and use this to baste the leg every time you twist it.

Replenish the fire as needed to keep it hot. Roast until the leg reaches an internal temperature of 53°C–56°C / 128°F–133°F for medium rare, 57°C–60°C / 135°F–140°F for medium.

Carefully remove the leg (by the string) to a wire rack set over a rimmed baking tray. Tent loosely with foil and rest for 10–15 minutes before carving.

SWEET POTATO AND THREE-MUSTARD COLCANNON

Serves 6

1kg / 2¼lb sweet potatoes, peeled and cut into 5cm / 2in cubes

500g / 1lb 2oz mustard greens (about 2 bunches), washed, ribbed and torn into 5cm / 2in pieces

120ml / 4fl oz / ½ cup double (heavy) cream

90g / 3oz / 6 tbsp butter

3 tbsp Lakeshore wholegrain mustard (or other wholegrain mustard, not coarse ground)

1 tbsp Dijon mustard

sea salt and ground white pepper

Place sweet potato pieces in a steamer set above 10cm / 4in of water at a rolling boil. Steam for 15 minutes, until soft enough to be cut with the back of a table knife.

Place torn mustard greens in a deep bowl with 1 tablespoon of sea salt and cover with boiling water. Let steep for 2 minutes, stirring occasionally. Drain, shock in ice water, drain when cold and spin dry.

Place cream, butter and wholegrain mustard in a small saucepan over medium–low heat to melt butter. Bring to a simmer.

Mash cooked sweet potatoes by hand until smooth. Stir in blanched mustard greens. Stir in Dijon mustard. Pour in cream/butter/mustard mixture and stir to combine.

Season with salt and white pepper to taste and more butter and mustards if desired.

FUCHSIA SHORTBREAD WITH DINGLE GIN LEMON CURD

Serves 6

For the fuchsia sugar:

50g / 1¾oz / ¼ cup granulated sugar

1 handful (about ½ cup) fresh organic fuchsia flowers

For the shortbread:

50g / 1¾oz / ½ cup jumbo (old-fashioned) rolled oats

210g / 7½oz / 1¾ cups plain (all-purpose) flour

40g / 1½oz / ¼ cup cornflour (cornstarch)

80g / 2¾oz / ⅔ cup icing (powdered) sugar

½ tsp table salt

210g / 7½oz / 14 tbsp unsalted butter, chilled and cut into slices 3mm / ⅛in thick

For the lemon curd:

165ml / 5½ oz / ⅔ cup lemon juice – from about 4 lemons

4 large eggs

2 egg yolks

200g / 7oz / 1 cup granulated sugar

60g / 2oz / 4 tbsp unsalted butter, chilled and cut into 1cm / ½in cubes

2 tbsp Dingle Original Gin

pinch of table salt

To decorate:

fresh fruit or fresh mint leaves

In an airtight container, mix sugar and fuchsia flowers. Shake twice per day for three or four days. Sift out flowers and reserve sugar for dusting shortbreads orother uses (great in tea, if you're one of the unholy, like myself).

> *Chef's tip:*
> *Fuchsia grows in nearly every hedgerow here in Dingle. Make sure that the flowers you collect haven't been sprayed with pesticides or chemical fertilisers. The potted variety work fine but, again, make sure they are not sprayed!*

Preheat the oven to 220°C / 430°F / gas mark 8. Line an ungreased 23cm / 9in round cake tin with non-stick baking paper cut to fit.

Pulse oats in spice grinder or blender until reduced to fine powder, about ten 5-second pulses.

In bowl of stand mixer fitted with paddle attachment, mix oat flour, plain flour, cornflour, icing sugar and salt on low speed until combined, about 5 seconds. Add butter to dry ingredients and continue to mix on low speed until a crumbly dough just forms and pulls away from sides of bowl, 5–7 minutes.

Remove bowl from mixer and toss mixture lightly with fingers to fluff and loosen. Rub any remaining butter bits into flour mixture with fingertips.

Turn half of crumbs into the lined cake tin, evening the crumbs gently with fingertips. Press down firmly with a second cake tin. Add remaining crumbs, even and press as with the first half of crumbs. Working quickly, smooth top of dough with back of spoon.

Insert paring knife between dough and pan. Leaving knife stationary so as not to tear the dough, rotate pan towards the sharp edge to free edges of dough.

Unmould dough onto an inverted baking tray lined with non-stick baking paper by placing the lined tray on top of the cake tin, inverting and then removing the tin. Peel baking paper from the top of the dough and smooth edges if necessary.

Place 5cm / 2in metal biscuit cutter in centre of dough and cut out centre. Place the cut round to one side, then replace the empty biscuit cutter in the hole.

Place shortbread in oven and immediately reduce temperature to 150°C / 300°F / gas mark 2.

Bake for 20 minutes. Remove baking tray from oven and score top surface of shortbread into 16 even wedges with a thin knife, then, using a wooden skewer, pierce each wedge 12 times in desired design. Sprinkle with 2 teaspoons of fuchsia sugar.

Return shortbread to oven and continue to bake until pale golden, about 40 minutes longer. Slide parchment with shortbread onto cutting board, remove cutter from centre, sprinkle with additional 2 teaspoons of fuchsia sugar.

Cut through the shortbread at scored marks into wedges. Slide baking paper with shortbread onto wire rack and cool to room temperature, at least 3 hours. (Can now be wrapped well and stored at room temperature for up to 7 days.)

To make the lemon curd, in a small, non-reactive saucepan over medium–high heat, warm the lemon juice until hot.

In a medium non-reactive bowl with a wet tea towel coiled under for stability, whisk eggs and yolks to combine. Slowly whisk in sugar. Whisking constantly and vigorously, slowly pour hot lemon juice into the egg mixture.

Return the juice and egg mixture to the saucepan and replace on medium heat. Stir constantly with a wooden spoon so that it does not curdle until the mixture registers 76°C / 170°F on an instant-read thermometer and is thick enough to cling to spoon, about 3 minutes (the spoon will leave a clear trail in the bottom of the saucepan for a moment or two when the curd is ready).

Remove pan from heat and stir in cold butter one or two pieces at a time, until nearly melted, then add the next pieces until all are incorporated. Stir in Dingle gin and salt.

Strain the lemon curd through a fine-mesh strainer into small non-reactive bowl. Cover with cling film pressed directly on the surface of curd to prevent a skin forming and refrigerate for up to three days.

To serve, arrange shortbread wedges on a dessert plate along with a big dollop of lemon curd. Garnish with fresh fruit or mint as desired.

DENIS O'CONNOR
The Half Door

DINING WITH FRIENDS

Catching up with Denis O'Connor while he catches up with the morning papers

L IKE MANY KIDS in an Irish farm family of seven children, Denis O'Connor knew what proper food looked like, what it tasted like and had at least an inkling of how it should be cooked. When someone, in their wisdom, offered his class a chance to leave school for the day and interview for CERT – the former state tourism training agency – most members of the class, Denis included, took the day away from preparing for the Leaving Certificate. Thus began the storied career of the Kanturk, County Cork man, now owner of the Half Door Restaurant in Dingle.

Two years at Rockwell Catering College in the early 1980s eventually led to jobs in London hotels in kitchens with 200-plus chefs. With an upward trajectory that could have landed him a top job in short order, Denis came to Kerry to take a second-chef job that within a year turned into head chef at the Towers Hotel in Glenbeigh. Best of all, this was where he met Teresa, his wife – a Glenbeigh native – and they headed back to London for more hotel work.

When Denis's dad passed away, he and Teresa came back to Ireland to be close to family. That led the couple to the Skellig, which had just reopened after a stint in receivership, where Denis was to be the new head chef and Teresa worked front of house. It was a new chapter for the hotel and for the couple.

Winters were quiet in Dingle back in those days. With the hotel closed from October until Good Friday, it was off to Florida for a couple of winters to work in an American seafood restaurant and sharing a rented house with two retired priests. I imagine that Denis has a book full of stories about those two seasons abroad.

After three years of heading up the Skellig, Denis wanted to be closer to some of his siblings who had emigrated to Australia, so the couple got residency visas and moved down under. But that same longing for family, coupled with the distance between Melbourne and Kerry, was too much for Teresa. They came back to Dingle and were able to get back into their former roles, as the head chef job had yet to be filled.

In 1991, the Half Door, which had been a standard-bearer of the Dingle culinary landscape since it opened in 1977, went up for sale. The couple jumped at the chance to own and operate a place for themselves.

As Denis told me as we sat at the bar of the seasonally quiet restaurant, 'When you get a new home, you get a new chick.' Within two weeks of opening their version of the Half Door, Teresa was pregnant with the first of their three children.

Like many of the chefs who have come to fall in love with Dingle the town, Dingle the community and Dingle the food, Denis and Teresa (who now does much of the cooking in the kitchen) learned that the best way to serve the extraordinary produce of the peninsula is to source the best and to do as little to it as possible. 'You don't drown a black sole in butter and cream sauce – they'd have your head,' Denis told me, speaking of both the local clientele as well the political and entertainment elite known to Denis as regular customers and more often as friends.

The fact that a second generation of the Half Door's suppliers are still coming in for lunch and dinner says it better than anything else. The people who supply the highest quality know where to have it cooked simply, properly and tastefully and served with a friendly smile.

Though much of the O'Connor family's entertaining is done at the restaurant, which serves as a de facto family dining room, for those times when they do have friends or colleagues over for a light meal and conversation, it's fresh, simple food that does them best. Find the freshest ingredients and don't get in their way.

WEEKNIGHT WITH THE NEIGHBOURS

starter
Scallop bisque

main
Oven-baked side of wild salmon

side
Roasted asparagus

dessert
Wild chestnut honey crème brûlée

cocktail suggestion
Inverted Lillet Martini (page 258)

wine suggestion
Australian Semillon-Sauvignon Blanc blend

Though little is more satisfying to a busy soul than sitting down with friends for a simple meal in comfortable surroundings, trying to fit it all in can be difficult – especially the cooking part. Denis's remedy for that is to offer a salmon dish that pretty much cooks in the residual heat of the roasted asparagus while you set the table and open a bottle of crisp white wine. If you'd like a sauce with your salmon, Stella Doyle's salsa verde (page 28) can be made in advance or whipped up in a few minutes.

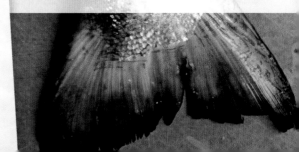

SCALLOP BISQUE

Serves 6

For the stock:

3kg (6¾lb) white fish bones and trimmings (from a non-oily fish)

3 carrots, peeled and quartered

3 onions, peeled and quartered

3 celery stalks, quartered

1 garlic clove, halved

2 floury potatoes, peeled and quartered

1 bottle Muscadet or other dry white wine

2 fresh bay leaves

1 bunch of fresh parsley, washed

½ lemongrass stalk, coarsely chopped

6 black peppercorns

1 tbsp sea salt

Cold water

For the bisque:

15g (1 tbsp) butter

2 tbsp extra virgin olive oil

680g (1lb 8oz) large sea scallops, cleaned and patted dry

370ml / 13fl oz / 1½ cups double (heavy) cream

1 tbsp snipped fresh chives, to garnish

Chef's tip: Make extra fish stock and freeze for up to 6 months. Once you have it on hand, you'll be surprised how often you'll use it.

In a very large stockpot, combine fish bones and trimmings with carrots, onions, celery, garlic, potatoes, wine, bay leaves, parsley, lemongrass, salt and peppercorns with enough cold water to cover – about 3 litres / 5¼ pints / 12 cups. Bring to a hard simmer over medium–high heat, skim off the foam, lower heat to medium–low and cook for 40 minutes. Strain through a colander into a clean stockpot. Return to a simmer until reduced by half.

In a large, heavy frying pan over a high heat, melt butter and olive oil together until very hot but not smoking. Sear scallops about 1 minute on each side. Set aside.

Deglaze the pan with 250ml / 9fl oz / 1 cup of the stock, scrape up the bits and add back to the simmering stock.

Strain stock through a fine-mesh strainer into a heavy-bottomed saucepan. Add cream. Simmer until slightly thickened, about 15 minutes.

Cut the scallops into three or four slices each and arrange in warm serving bowls. Adjust seasoning of the bisque, pour over scallop slices. Garnish with chives.

OVEN-BAKED SIDE OF WILD SALMON

Serves 6–8 depending on the size of the fillets

1–2 wild salmon fillets (depending on size)
1 potato, scrubbed
1 lemon, sliced 3mm / ⅛in thick
1 baby fennel bulb, thinly sliced
2–4 tsp extra virgin olive oil
salt and freshly ground black pepper

Preheat the oven to 260°C / 500°F / gas mark 10. Place a rimmed baking tray in the oven to preheat too.

Place salmon, skin side down, on a piece of non-stick baking paper cut to fit the preheating pan.

For each fillet, cut two slices of potato, one slightly thicker than the other. Put the thicker slice under the tail end and the other a bit further up the fillet, in order to make it roast evenly. Rub the fillet with oil.

Cut through the peel and into the flesh of each lemon slice. Carefully remove the skin from the flesh. Squeeze the juice into a bowl and reserve. With a very sharp paring knife, remove most of the bitter, white pith from the zest and discard. Tie the zests into individual single knots.

Season the salmon with salt and pepper, scatter fennel slices on and around the fillet(s) and then place the lemon knots on the fillet(s).

Carefully pick up the paper holding the salmon and place on the preheated tray. Reduce heat to 135°C / 275°F / gas mark 1. Roast until salmon reaches 52°C / 125°F for medium rare and a bit higher if you like your salmon more well done. (This can be done as soon as asparagus comes out of the oven.)

Remove and sprinkle with reserved lemon juice and serve on the baking tray with roasted asparagus scattered around the fillet.

ROASTED ASPARAGUS

Serves 6

3 tbsp olive oil
2 garlic cloves, finely chopped
1 tsp chopped fresh thyme leaves
salt and freshly ground black pepper
650g / 1lb 7oz asparagus, tough ends trimmed
1 red bell pepper, cored, seeded and thinly sliced
5 shallots, thinly sliced
1½ tbsp red wine vinegar

Preheat the oven to 260°C / 500°F / gas mark 10.

Stir oil, garlic, thyme, ½ teaspoon salt and ¼ teaspoon pepper together in large bowl. Spread asparagus across rimmed baking tray, drizzle with half of garlic mixture and toss to coat.

Rearrange asparagus in single layer. Combine bell pepper and shallots with remaining garlic mixture in bowl and toss to coat. Scatter pepper and shallots evenly over asparagus.

Roast until asparagus begins to soften and turns bright green with some dark brown edges, about 8 minutes.

Drizzle with vinegar and continue roasting until asparagus is softened and bell pepper and shallots begin to brown at the edges, 3–5 minutes. Remove from oven (and place salmon in if using along with roasted salmon, remembering to reduce heat to 135°C / 275°F / gas mark 1).

Toss vegetables, season with salt and pepper. Serve with roast salmon fillet.

Chef's tip:
Those tough ends
and any peelings
from asparagus work
very well in soup
as you'll purée and
strain anyway. Don't
throw away such
flavourful bits.

WILD CHESTNUT HONEY CRÈME BRÛLÉE

Serves 8

500ml / 18fl oz / 2 cups cream
120ml / 4fl oz / ½ cup milk
1 vanilla bean, split lengthwise
8 egg yolks
120ml / 4fl oz / ½ cup wild chestnut honey
50g / 1¾oz / ¼ cup turbinado sugar (see Chef's Tip on page 12)

Preheat the oven to 150°C / 300°F / gas mark 2.

In a small, non-reactive saucepan over medium heat, add cream and milk. Scrape seeds from vanilla bean into cream and add empty pod. Bring nearly to a boil – when bubbles start to form around the edge – and remove to cool.

In a mixing bowl, whisk yolks and honey until pale yellow and light, about 3 minutes.

Continue whisking, slowly adding hot cream (do this slowly so not to scramble the yolks). When you have added about half of the cream, reverse the process and stir the yolk and cream mixture into the remaining cream in the saucepan. Return to heat for just a moment as you stir to combine completely. Remove from heat.

Line the bottom of a roasting tin with a clean tea towel. Arrange 8 x 180ml / 6fl oz / ¾ cup ramekins inside the tin. Divide the custard evenly among the ramekins.

Boil a kettle of water and pour enough boiling water into the tin to come halfway up the sides of the ramekins.

Bake the custards until set but slightly loose in centre, about 35 minutes.

Remove the roasting tin from the oven, and, using tongs, transfer the ramekins to a wire rack to cool completely. Refrigerate until firm, at least 4 hours and up to two days.

To serve, sprinkle about 2 teaspoons of sugar evenly over the surface of each custard. Using a kitchen blowtorch, melt and 'burn' the sugar until bubbly and dark brown. Let stand for 1 minute to allow sugar to harden before serving.

Gambas pil-pil (see page 75)

SEAN ROCHE

Doyle's Seafood Restaurant

ONLY THE BEST

Sean Roche's goal is the pitch-perfect dinner party

FROM MIDLETON IN COUNTY CORK, Sean Roche and his sister, Sinéad, grew up in a family that appreciated quality food and wine and they had been coming to Dingle on holidays with their parents since they were children. I mention Sinéad because she, too, is a fixture in the foodscape of Dingle, as she owns Ashe's Bar and Restaurant not far from Sean's Doyle's Seafood Restaurant. Sean entered the industry in 1998 – 6 April 1998, Sean recalls exactly – in his mother's first cousin's restaurant when he was just thirteen years old and he's never looked back. Having long-established contacts-cum-friendships here in Dingle, his father set him up with a summer gig working in Pat Moore's Beginish. After his Leaving Cert exams, he came back to Dingle to work and continue his hands-on culinary training.

Following the route of young Sean's early cooking career wouldn't be a bad way to plan a holiday: Kinsale, Galway, Paris, Cork, Donegal, London, Dublin, Dingle. He has worked in some of the best restaurants in Ireland, in four-star hotels and a few Michelin-star kitchens to round out the experience.

His first go at running his own kitchen was at the luxury Castle Grove Country House Hotel in Letterkenny, County Donegal (a property that once belonged to the British royal family) when he was just twenty-one. However, it takes a seriously mature mind to leave an ego-feeding head chef job for more experience. 'I knew I had to get my arse kicked,' Sean told me. He took a 75 per cent cut in pay in order to see ingredients and techniques that were not being used in Ireland ... yet; so it was off to London.

While the likes of lemongrass, lime leaves, baby gem lettuce, kohlrabi and salsify are found in many good grocers around the island now, in the days on the cusp of the early Celtic Tiger years, even the most sophisticated houses along what is now the Wild Atlantic Way weren't using ingredients that adventurous. On his days off from the Four Seasons London Hotel, Sean showed up at the back door of the best kitchens in the city with his knife kit and chef's whites in hand to volunteer his time in order to learn as much as he could.

'Have you not had a look around the place?' was Sean's answer when I asked why he finally landed in Dingle. He's a country boy at heart, and as he says, 'Dingle is not just a place.' It may have been the draw to get him here, but the people, the professionals and the ingredients of the peninsula are what keep a chef in Dingle.

If Sean or one of the surrounding restaurateurs gets a delivery while they are out of the kitchen, a neighbour will receive and store the goods for them. Short an item for service? Half a case of butter is likely to be lent the way a cup of sugar might be borrowed over a hedge. If one dining room is full for the night, customers are guided to one of the other fine establishments in town. That sort of thing just doesn't happen in many places in our industry. Dingle is special.

After nearly thirty years in kitchens, food isn't just a job or a profession for Sean. It's his passion. Sean was also one of the chefs that brought the now-famous Dingle Food Festival to life in 2006.

His holidays are usually planned around experiencing ingredients, preparations and presentations of foods from around the world, perhaps with a round of golf or two thrown in for the craic. It's also a passion that he is passing to his young son, also named Sean. If his plans to become a professional soccer player don't come through, cheffing is his second choice of career. It's not uncommon to find them foraging, shopping, preparing and cooking a meal together on Sean's days off. The youngest Roche can roll his own pasta, eats his steaks rare and can put away tapas like a champion. A passion for the best and finest has assuredly passed to the next generation of the Roche family.

A TASTE OF SPANISH HOLIDAYS

starters
Grilled oysters with herb butter

Gambas pil pil

main
Spanish-style fish stew

dessert
Sticky toffee pudding

cocktail suggestion
Ginito (page 256)

wine suggestion
Albariño from Galicia

Sean isn't the only chef who loves the idea of small plates for his own dining, so he has offered two starters from his Spanish holiday memories. Add Lee Sim's crab mayonnaise (page 244) and you could do without the stew altogether. Or scrap the starters and serve the fish stew with Martin Bealin's oatcakes (page 88), local cheeses and his three-onion jam (page 87) and the stew will stand alone as a steaming one-pot meal for any day or night.

GRILLED OYSTERS WITH HERB BUTTER

Serves 6

18 oysters, shucked

200g / 7oz / 2 cups finely grated mature Cheddar cheese

For the tomato compote:

100ml / 3½fl oz / ⅓ cup + 4 tsp extra virgin olive oil

1 small onion, finely chopped

2 garlic cloves, crushed

150g / 5¼oz canned chopped tomatoes

1 tbsp tomato purée (paste)

50g / 1¾oz / ¼ cup sugar

60ml / 2fl oz / ¼ cup red wine vinegar

1 bay leaf

salt and freshly ground black pepper

For the herb butter:

1 to 1½ bunches (about 150g / 5¼oz) wild garlic leaves or garlic chives

150g / 5¼oz rocket (arugula)

1 to 1½ bunches (about 150g / 5¼oz) fresh flat-leaf parsley, picked, plus extra to garnish

75g / 2½oz fresh chives

1 garlic clove

450g / 1lb soft butter

½ lemon, juiced

Preheat the oven to 180°C / 350°F / gas mark 4.

Shuck the oysters, but keep and clean the bottom shell for serving.

For the tomato compote, heat the oil in a heavy-bottomed saucepan over medium heat and sauté onion and garlic with a pinch of sea salt until soft but not coloured. Add the tomatoes and purée, sugar, vinegar and bay leaf. Reduce heat to low and cook gently, stirring occasionally, for 30 minutes.

While the sauce is simmering, place all the herbs and garlic in a food processor with seasoning and pulse two or three times. Add the butter and lemon juice, pulse three or four times then blend completely. Correct the seasoning with salt and pepper to taste.

On a large tray, place three large sheets of squashed tin foil in rows to balance the oyster shells. In the bottom of each shell place a small amount of the tomato compote, followed by one oyster and then a small amount of the cheese, then top this with a good amount (about 2 teaspoons) of the herb butter. Place in oven for 6 minutes, then remove and place under a hot grill (broiler) for 3–4 minutes. Garnish with fresh parsley leaves.

GAMBAS PIL PIL

Serves 6

36 fresh large gambas (shrimp, or prawns, as photographed), deveined

3 large fresh chillies, sliced (cayenne or Kung Pao work well)

6 large garlic cloves, sliced

6 large garlic cloves, crushed

1 tbsp Maldon sea salt flakes

1 tbsp crushed black peppercorns

350ml / 12fl oz / 1⅓ cups extra virgin Spanish olive oil

2 tbsp chopped fresh parsley

Preheat the oven to 180°C / 350°F / gas mark 4. Warm six pil pil dishes (or small gratin dishes) in the oven.

Place all the ingredients except parsley in a large saucepan over medium–high heat and cook gently, stirring once in a while, until the shrimp are just cooked through, about 3 minutes.

Remove the dishes from the oven – be careful, as they will be hot. Divide the shrimp evenly between them (six each) and top with 2–3 tablespoons of the cooking oil. Garnish with parsley.

Chef's tip:
How you treat garlic – slice, crush, mince, chop – will affect the flavour of your finished dish. Using both sliced and crushed garlic, this dish will have the sharp bite from the crushed, and the warm, toasted garlic flavour from the sliced garlic.

SPANISH-STYLE FISH STEW

Serves 6–8

1 medium onion, sliced

10 garlic cloves, crushed

2 celery stalks, chopped

1 fennel bulb, sliced

1 leek, sliced

60ml / 2fl oz / ¼ cup Spanish olive oil

chilli powder or cayenne pepper, to taste

3 tbsp paella spice

2 tsp smoked paprika

¼ tsp saffron powder

¼ tsp saffron threads

300ml / ½ pint / 1¼ cups white wine

2 tbsp tomato purée (paste)

1 x 400g / 14oz can of plum tomatoes, chopped

2 bay leaves

500ml / 18fl oz / 2 cups fresh fish stock or equivalent amount of reconstituted fish bouillon

Tabasco, to taste

Lea & Perrins Worcestershire sauce, to taste

1 tbsp coriander seeds

2 star anise

1kg / 2¼lb mixed shellfish, such as mussels, clams, prawns, crab, cockles, scallops

1kg / 2¼lb mixed fish, such as monkfish, turbot, salmon, calamari, hake, halibut, cut into bite-sized pieces

250ml / 9fl oz / 1 cup Verdelho or other Spanish dry white wine

12g / ¾oz / ½ cup fresh herbs such as basil, coriander (cilantro), parsley, chives and/or chervil, chopped

1 bunch of spring onions (scallions), thinly sliced

salt and freshly ground black pepper

crusty bread, to serve

In a large, heavy-bottomed pot set over medium–high heat, sauté all vegetables in olive oil with a pinch of salt until soft but not browned. Remove from heat, add spices and cook in the residual heat of the pan for 2 minutes, stirring constantly.

Return to heat, add wine and reduce by half. Add tomato purée and plum tomatoes and bring to a boil. Add bay leaves and fish stock (if using powder, be careful that it won't get too salty), Tabasco and Worcestershire sauce to taste. Add coriander seeds and star anise and bring to a simmer. Lower heat to medium and simmer for 10–12 minutes. This is your base sauce and will keep in the refrigerator for a few days or you can freeze it if you wish.

Steam shellfish in a steamer basket over wine and 250ml / 9fl oz / 1 cup water until just cooked. Remove and place on a large plate.

Turn off heat and place all fish into the shellfish-steaming liquid. Stir gently and poach for 2–3 minutes. Remove fish with slotted spoon to a plate.

Heat tomato base and fish-poaching liquid to a boil in a large pot over medium–high heat. Add shellfish and stir. Bring back to a simmer and add fish. Stir and remove from heat.

Add spring onions and fresh herbs and serve in large warmed bowls with lots of crusty bread.

STICKY TOFFEE PUDDING

Serves 8

For the puddings:

160g / 5½oz / ⅔ cup pitted dates, roughly chopped

180ml / 6fl oz / ¾ cup warm water + ¼ tsp baking soda

80g / 2¾oz / ⅔ cup pitted dates, sliced about 5mm / ¼in thick

150g / 5¼oz / ¾ cup well-packed dark brown sugar

2 large eggs

1¾ tsp vanilla extract

60g / 2oz / 4 tbsp unsalted butter, melted

½ tsp table salt

160g / 5½oz / 1¼ cups plain (all-purpose) flour, sifted

½ tsp baking powder

30g / 1oz / 2 tbsp butter, for greasing

For the toffee sauce:

110g / 4oz / 1 stick unsalted butter

200g / 7oz / 1 cup dark brown sugar

2 tbsp Dingle Distillery whiskey

150ml / 5¼fl oz / ⅔ cup cream

1 tsp finely grated lemon zest

Chef's tip: Soaking the dates in baking-soda water softens the tough skins and makes for a creamy texture.

Preheat the oven to 180°C / 350°F / gas mark 4.

To make the puddings, mix the chopped dates with the warm water and baking soda. Soak, stirring now and again, for 5 minutes. Drain (reserving the liquid) and place softened dates into a small bowl.

Place sliced dates in a large bowl with about half the brown sugar and mash with a fork until mostly incorporated. Add remaining sugar, eggs, vanilla, and reserved soaking liquid to date / sugar mixture and stir until well mixed. Stir melted butter into mixture. Fold in softened dates and salt.

Sift flour and baking powder together into a second bowl. Mix dry ingredients into the wet mixture.

Set the kettle on to boil. Divide batter between eight greased ramekins (they'll be about half full). Place puddings on top of a clean tea towel in a large roasting tin with sides at least 5cm / 2in high but no more than 10cm / 4in.

Pour boiling water from kettle into the roasting tin, taking care not to get water in the puddings, to reach the level of the puddings inside their ramekins. Cover pan with a tight-fitting lid or wrap tightly with foil. Bake until the puddings look like pancakes ready to flip (bubbles have burst, leaving small holes), which should take 30–50 minutes, depending on the day. Remove to a clean, dry tea towel on the counter and allow them to cool in their moulds.

To make the toffee sauce, melt the butter in a heavy-bottomed saucepan over low heat. Increase heat to medium and stir in brown sugar. Cook and continue to stir until smooth, dissolved and beginning to darken.

Take off heat and stir in whiskey (take particular care if you are near a naked flame, as the booze can ignite). Return to low heat and whisk in cream in a slow, steady stream. Stir until sauce just begins to froth, but not until it boils, for it will easily curdle (about 3 minutes). Keep warm.

To serve, run a thin blade around each pudding and invert onto a dessert plate. Top with a few tablespoons of sauce.

MARTIN BEALIN

The Global Village

HOME AND ABROAD

*Digging up great dinner ideas in
Martin's polytunnel garden*

CHEF MARTIN BEALIN grew up on a sheep farm in the Wicklow Mountains. Looking back on the food of his childhood, Martin smiles and tells me that everything they ate was free range, organic and hormone-free because that's just how things were in that time and place. It wasn't a fad: 'It's just how you grow things if you want them to taste like they're supposed to!' he said.

Today, Martin employs a full-time farmer to supply his multi-award-winning restaurant, the Global Village, but he remembers cutting hay by hand with a scythe as a boy and he still enjoys getting his hands into the soil when he has the time. It's likely that it is purity of flavour – that memory of what real food tasted like – not fashion, that drives Martin to grow much of his menu and source the rest locally.

While he was studying to be an engineer, he worked in pubs and restaurants to put himself through university. He first got a taste of working with food that hadn't been raised by his own family when he worked in a takeaway owned by a friend's father, and he then worked with a number of 'proper chefs' as his interest in engineering waned.

He left his studies and went into an intensive residential culinary programme at the Great Southern Hotel in Rosslare. Trained in the classics of French cuisine, Martin still cringes at the amount of chips served alongside 1980s Irish haute cuisine.

Like everybody in the industry did at the time, upon qualification as a chef, Martin left Ireland to explore a world beyond meat and two veg. From a massive hotel operation in Jersey in the Channel Islands, where he learned that there were places in the world that treat chefs as professionals, he followed a talented chef who could trace his training lineage directly back to Georges Auguste Escoffier, 'the king of chefs and chef of kings', about 30 miles north-west to a new restaurant in Guernsey. That's where Martin really started to learn.

During off-seasons, he and his fellow chefs from Guernsey would travel to other seasonal locations throughout Europe for work. In short order, Martin's travels shifted from travelling to work with food to travelling for his love of food. Backpacking and campervan travels to market towns and fishing ports, small farms and artisan food producers in and around Europe then led him to working travels throughout South-East Asia and Australia as well as Central and South America, where it wasn't uncommon for him to follow his nose into a home kitchen to see what was cooking and to learn from local family cooks.

Martin now laughs at the fact that he was taken off more than a few buses at gunpoint as he travelled through war zones in his decade-long pursuit of culinary adventure, but working a series of seasonal jobs in different places around the globe fostered an understanding of the importance of the seasonality of ingredients as well as the changing cooking methods used on the same produce as the seasons change. The seeds of Martin's global cooking were planted deep and tended well.

Like many Irish chefs who had emigrated to better-paying gigs around the world, Martin came back to Ireland as the boom times were beginning. Dipping his toe in the water by working as an agency chef, he filled in at quality kitchens around Dublin and then all the way down to Kerry.

At the end of a short stint in Waterville, he phoned the agency to tell them he was heading back to Dublin when they diverted him to Dingle – like so many others, to the Dingle Skellig Hotel. The rest, as they say, is history.

On a split-shift break, Martin strolled past a vacant shop at the top of the main street that, he told a mate, 'would make a nice restaurant', and thus, a few short weeks later, the Global Village was born.

'The Global', as it's called by friends, has evolved over the years and is now one of the reasons that people come from around the world to visit the food destination that Dingle has become. Some of the best chefs in the country have trained and worked in Martin's kitchen. He even met his wife, Nuala, at the Global in 1997 when she ate Martin's traditionally cooked basmati rice. Apparently it's not only a man's heart that can be won through the stomach.

Martin's personal and professional ethos was 'think globally, act locally' long before it was a popular catchphrase. The menu he offers speaks that in volumes.

Martin likes to take the highest-quality local produce and infuse it with international flavours and ingredients. The warm and wonderful cooking smells that will waft from your kitchen as you simmer crab shells and roast spiced lamb will make the neighbours jealous of the guests arriving for your dinner party. Rachael Boyle's coriander naan bread (page 155) fits this menu perfectly. If you'd prefer something sweet to finish rather than Martin's offering of local cheeses, try Denis O'Connor's chestnut honey crème brûlée (page 67) to keep with the warm Mediterranean theme.

A COOK'S ATLAS

starter
Crab and Dingle whiskey bisque

main
Slow-roast shoulder of salt grass lamb with Moorish spices and stuffing

side
Perfect basmati rice pilaf

dessert
Local cheeses with oatcakes and caramelised onion jam

suggestion

CRAB AND DINGLE WHISKEY BISQUE

Serves 6

1kg / 2¼lb / 6 cups crab shells and bodies, broken and chopped
120ml / 4fl oz / ½ cup Dingle whiskey
1 onion, roughly chopped
1 carrot, roughly chopped
2 tbsp tomato purée (paste)
2 sprigs of fresh thyme
6 sprigs of fresh parsley
570g / 20oz canned chopped tomatoes
2 fresh bay leaves
12 black peppercorns
cold water, to cover
5 drops of Tabasco sauce

In a tall heavy-based pot, crush the crab shells with the end of a rolling pin – this is to extract more flavour while the shells are cooking. 'Roast' on a high heat and add the whiskey. Allow the alcohol to cook off for about 3 minutes before adding the remainder of the ingredients (except the Tabasco sauce) and enough water to cover the shells. Boil for 30 minutes, then reduce to a simmer for a further hour.

Drain the liquid through a fine-mesh strainer to remove all sediment and traces of shell. Pour the liquid into a fresh pot and return to a low heat to allow the flavour to become enhanced and the bisque to become reduced and thicken.

To finish the bisque add some seasoning and the Tabasco. The bisque needs to be tasted regularly throughout the cooking process to check the salt content. Add only a little salt when seasoning.

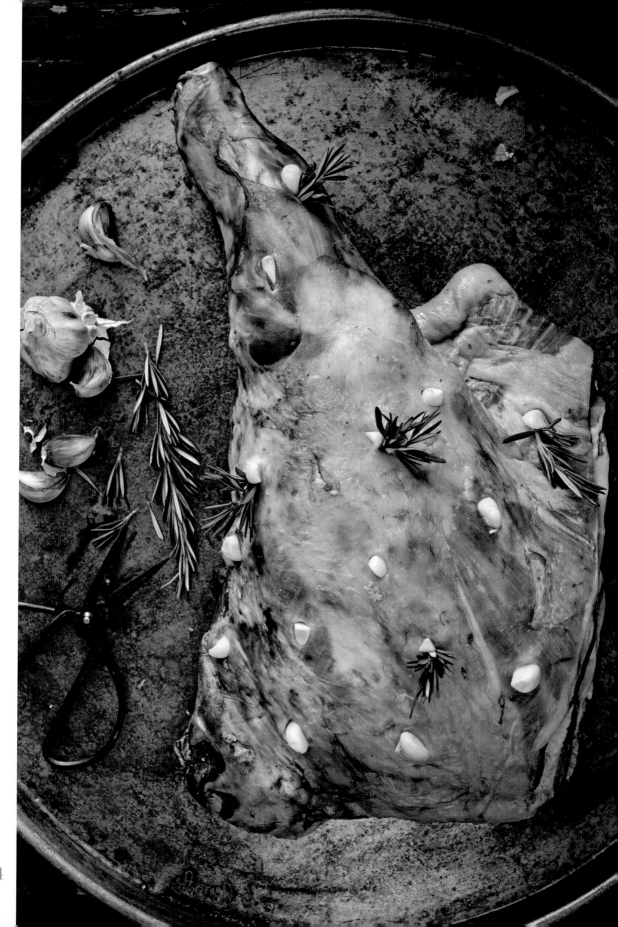

SLOW-ROAST SHOULDER OF SALT GRASS LAMB WITH MOORISH SPICES AND STUFFING

Serves 6–8

120ml / 4fl oz / ½ cup extra virgin olive oil

25g / ¾oz / ¼ cup ras el hanout spice

2 garlic cloves, sliced

1 tbsp sea salt

1 tsp ground white pepper

1 shoulder of lamb – have your butcher bone the shoulder, but keep the bones for stock

reserved stems of parsley and coriander (cilantro) from the stuffing, finely chopped

2 garlic cloves, crushed

1 tsp coarse sea salt

For the stuffing:

4 tbsp olive oil

60g / 2oz / 4 tbsp butter

1 onion, finely chopped

2 garlic cloves, crushed

1 small handful (¼ cup) parsley leaves, chopped (reserve the stems)

1 small handful (¼ cup) coriander (cilantro) leaves, chopped (reserve the stems)

1 tsp fresh thyme leaves

360g / 12½oz / 3 cups fresh breadcrumbs

salt and freshly ground black pepper

60g / 2oz / 4 tbsp butter, melted – as needed

110g / 4oz / ½ cup dried apricots, quartered

60g / 2oz / ½ cup slivered almonds

60g / 2oz dry-cured chorizo, finely chopped

In a small saucepan, warm the oil, ras el hanout and sliced garlic over medium–low heat for about 15 minutes to infuse oil. Add salt and white pepper. Remove and allow to cool completely.

Rub the lamb with spiced oil. Make sure to get oil into every bit of the lamb. Marinate, covered in the refrigerator, overnight.

Remove marinated lamb from refrigerator and let it come up to room temperature for an hour or two.

For the stuffing, heat a heavy-bottomed pan over medium heat. Add olive oil and butter and heat until the butter stops foaming. Add onion with a pinch of salt and cook until soft. Add garlic and cook for 30 seconds, until fragrant. Remove from heat and stir in herbs. Stir in breadcrumbs and season to taste.

Use the additional melted butter to make stuffing into something of a paste, rather than dry crumbs. Add apricots, almonds and chorizo. Set aside to cool.

Make a paste of the finely chopped stems, crushed garlic and coarse salt. Rub this paste into both sides of the shoulder.

Preheat the oven to 100°C / 210°F / gas mark ¼.

Lay shoulder on a large cutting board or cleaned countertop, fat side down. Leaving about 8cm / 3in of a border on the top and bottom, spread stuffing evenly on the meat. Roll tightly from the bottom into a cylinder and tie about every 4cm / 1½in so that it is a nice tight roll.

Heat a roasting tin over medium–high heat on the hob (stovetop). Sear the lamb in a hot pan on all sides until evenly browned. There should be enough oil on the lamb to sear, but if not, add a bit to the pan. Pop it into the preheated oven and roast low and slow for about 5 hours.

Remove the lamb and rest it under a foil tent for about 15 minutes before slicing to serve. Separate fat from drippings and use juices to moisten the roast.

PERFECT BASMATI RICE PILAF

Serves 6

400g / 14oz / 2¼ cups basmati rice
830ml / 29fl oz / 3⅓ cups water
2 tsp sea salt
freshly ground black pepper
60g / 2oz / 4 tbsp unsalted butter (or vegetable oil if preferred)
1 medium onion, finely chopped

Rinse rice in several changes of water – using your hands to agitate grains gently to release starch – until water runs almost clear. Drain through a fine-mesh strainer, place over a bowl and set aside.

In a medium saucepan, covered, over medium–high heat, bring water to boil. Add salt and season with pepper. Cover to keep hot.

In a large saucepan over medium heat, melt butter until foam begins to subside, add onion and cook, stirring often, until softened, 3–4 minutes. Add rice and stir to coat grains with butter. Cook until edges of rice grains begin to turn translucent, 3–4 minutes. Stir hot seasoned water into rice, bring to a boil, then reduce heat to low. Cover, and simmer until all liquid is absorbed, 16–18 minutes.

Remove from heat. Remove lid, place a clean tea towel under the lid to absorb excess steam and replace the lid. Let stand for 10 minutes. Fluff rice with fork and serve.

CARAMELISED ONION JAM

Makes 4 small jars

1kg / 2¼lb sweet onions (Martin likes Brunswick, but any firm, sweet onion will do)
60ml / 2fl oz / ¼ cup Irish rapeseed oil
¼ tsp sea salt
1 tbsp brown sugar
2 oranges, zest and juice
2 tbsp redcurrant jelly
60ml / 2fl oz / ¼ cup Madeira
1 star anise (optional)
1 small dried chilli (optional)

Peel and slice onions thinly.

Heat oil in a large, heavy-bottomed pot over medium–low heat. Add onions and salt. Cook slowly, stirring often, until the liquid has evaporated and the onions begin to turn dark golden – as long as 1 hour.

Stir in brown sugar and orange zest. Continue to cook for about 5 more minutes, stirring, until onions become slightly sticky. Add orange juice and deglaze the pan.

Add redcurrant jelly, Madeira and the spices, if using, and cook over low heat for additional 20 minutes. Gently stir often, as it will have a tendency to stick and burn.

Jam can be cooled and refrigerated, covered, for about two weeks. For longer storage, place hot jam into sterilised jars, seal with sterilised lids and process in boiling water for 3 minutes to seal. Refrigerate after opening.

Chef's tip:
When caramelising onions it is important to use relatively low heat. You must slowly cook off the moisture from the whole slice before the sugars can caramelise. Doing this too quickly will cause the onions to scorch and burn. The result will be a sharp, bitter flavour rather than a warm, sweet, rich one.

OATCAKES

Makes 8

225g / 8oz / 2¼ cups jumbo (old-fashioned) rolled oats, plus extra for shaping
60g / 2oz / ¼ cup butter
120ml / 4fl oz / ½ cup buttermilk
75g / 2½oz / ½ cup plain (all-purpose) flour
½ tsp baking soda
¼ tsp cream of tartar
½ tsp table salt
2 tbsp light brown sugar

Preheat the oven to 180°C / 350°F / gas mark 4.

Place the oats in a large bowl.

In a small saucepan over medium heat, melt butter and buttermilk together until hot. (Buttermilk may curdle, but this is not an issue.)

In another bowl, sift together remaining ingredients. Combine with oats and make a well in the centre. Pour in the hot buttermilk and stir with a wooden spoon to moisten and combine.

Scatter additional oats on a countertop. Turn out dough and top with more oats. Pat into a 25cm / 10in circle about 5mm / ¼in thick, pressing hard (the bottom of a cake tin works well for this purpose).

Using a sharp chef's knife, cut into eight wedges. Carefully transfer to a baking tray lined with non-stick baking paper, leaving about 2.5cm / 1in between wedges, and place in oven. Reduce heat to 160°C / 320°F / gas mark 3 and bake for 30–40 minutes, until dark golden and firm.

Remove to wire rack to cool completely. Store in airtight container for up to one week. Serve with selection of cheeses, butter and onion marmalade.

Chef's tip: If the cakes need more time to dry, but you don't want them any darker, simply turn off the oven and let them finish using the residual heat.

JEAN-MARIE VAIREAUX

Out of the Blue

A CULINARY MERCENARY

*Trading chefs' whites and
a toque for motorcycle
leathers and a helmet,
Jean-Marie hits the road
on a rare afternoon off*

J EAN-MARIE VAIREAUX, a native of Lyon, France, spent his compulsory military service cooking for a four-star general in the French army, a man who had been captured a number of times in the Indochina wars. The general's one and only order to the kitchen staff was 'no chicken, no rice!' Jean-Marie got the comfortable post because he had just graduated from hotel school with the military detailer's son when his service was required. His culinary training began years earlier when he left the study of economics to pursue a passion set in motion in his grandparents' kitchen in an apartment block on the edge of the city.

Listening to Jean-Marie tell stories of his weekly trip to the *boucherie chevaline* to collect bavette steak for their tartare or how his grandfather parked his car on the street so that the small garage allotted to the flat could be used to store hardwood for the cooking stove, one can see why the young boy chose the pages of a menu rather than the pages of a textbook.

When he returned to work in the restaurant Le Panorama, where he began his apprenticeship in 1976, after the army, the chef/owner set the young man on a course that would eventually land him in Dingle. He sent the young commis chef on a series of short *stages* to butchers, fishmongers and patisseries as well as taking him to wholesale markets for produce, to see ice carvers and even to his private club, Chaîne des Rôtisseurs, where he smoked cigars with the likes of Paul Bocuse, La Grande Toque himself. This was the stuff of dreams for a young chef in training as he moved up the ranks of the brigade.

With the blessing and help of his old boss, the chef at Le Panorama, Jean-Marie and his new wife opened their own hotel with a bar and restaurant on the banks of the River Saône. Like many first-time chef/owners, he may have made this leap too soon in his career and the stresses of the hospitality business were too much for a new marriage. Though the place was quite successful, after a few years he sold the hotel and he and his wife divorced.

After a full year recovering from the experience by moping around his childhood home, it was the shoe of Jean-Marie's mother that kicked him back into the business.

After another few years working in the kitchens of successful Lyon restaurants and eventually a golf and country club, it was time for a change – a major change. Working somewhere with a cool climate was his number one priority, so in 1998, an advert for a now-defunct restaurant in Dingle lured the chef to pack his knives and a few belongings (and French cigarettes for his new boss, also a Frenchman) onto his beloved motorbike and head off to the wilds of west Kerry.

At 5:30 most mornings the two chefs were out on a boat, catching the day's menu of ray, mackerel, pollock and the occasional bass, then filleting them on upturned hulls in the boatyard. For lunch they would serve 150 to 200 people. Evening service was classic French seafood for another hundred or so.

Over the next decade and a half, Jean-Marie worked his way around all the best kitchens in the town. Spending a year or so in each restaurant, he lent his formidable talent, helping to grow the reputation of the peninsula as a culinary destination. His experience as a young chef learning in the speciality shops of Lyon served him well as he became Dingle's mercenary chef: have knives, will travel.

His first head chef taught Jean-Marie always to leave a job on good terms, and it's a mantra he has always held to. To this day he is respected around the kitchens of Dingle not only for his food and his work ethic, but also for his vast knowledge and his willingness to pitch in when needed. Dingle has also given back to him in the ingredients, like the variety of fresh fish he's been able to work with, that he didn't have in Lyon.

With his floppy chef's toque, he is a crowd favourite on the demonstration stage at every year's Dingle Food Festival, showing off one of his Kerry versions of a classic French preparation. He came for the weather (few people would say that of Ireland), but he stayed for the food, the professional opportunities and the challenges as well as for the fact that expectations and standards of food continue to rise here in Dingle. What more can a chef ask for?

Seaside dining with a scrubbed pine table, mismatched chairs, crazed old china, heavy silverware, sun-bleached table napkins, pink skin and salt in the air all come to mind when I read this menu. These fresh, clean flavours come from a past we may not share with the Frenchman, but I'd happily sit down to this meal any day of the week. Brian Heaton's buttery champ (page 219) would make a hearty side dish for this light seafood dinner party.

COASTAL COMFORT FOOD

starter
Scallop parcels in martini sauce

main
Mother's baked cod Provençal with aioli

side
Butter-toasted quinoa with petits pois

dessert
Baked lemon tart

cocktail suggestion
Hop, Skip & Go Naked (page 257)

wine suggestion
Rolle from Provence or
Vermentino from Sardinia (same grape)

SCALLOP PARCELS IN MARTINI SAUCE

Serves 6

1 head of Savoy cabbage

1 leek, dark green leaves only (reserve the white part for another use)

2–3 tbsp olive oil

6 large scallops, cleaned

60ml / 2fl oz / ¼ cup Dingle Original Gin

60ml / 2fl oz / ¼ cup dry vermouth

100g / 3½oz / ½ cup butter

2 shallots, finely chopped

250ml / 9fl oz / 1 cup double (heavy) cream

salt and freshly ground black pepper

2 tbsp finely chopped fresh parsley

Remove several outer leaves from head of cabbage to find light-coloured and tender leaves. Gently remove six of these leaves without tearing them.

In a large pot of salted water, par-cook the leaves of cabbage for 1–2 minutes to tenderise them. Drop into a large bowl of ice water to shock. Drain and pat dry with a clean tea towel. Cut the rib out of the leaves if they are large and tough.

Make leek ribbons by cutting 5mm / ¼in strips of leek greens into 15cm / 6in ribbons, then blanching in boiling water for 30 seconds before shocking in ice water. Pat dry.

In a sauté pan over medium–high heat, pour olive oil and heat until shimmering. Sear scallops for 30 seconds each side to brown – do not overcook. Remove pan from heat and add gin. Flambé for about 10 seconds and add vermouth. Remove scallops to a cold plate.

Add butter and shallots to the pan and sweat over low heat until soft with no colour – about 5 minutes. Add cream, increase heat to medium and reduce until sauce is silky. Remove from heat.

Place one scallop on each cabbage leaf and lightly season with salt and pepper. Pour 1 teaspoon of sauce over scallop, gather the leaf into a parcel and tie with leek ribbon.

Return parcels to sauce in the pan and simmer for 2–3 minutes, basting in sauce to heat. Serve in a martini glass with a little of the sauce. Garnish with parsley.

MOTHER'S BAKED COD PROVENÇAL WITH AIOLI

Serves 6

6 x 200g / 7oz cod fillets, skin on and thick near the head

1 bottle of dry white wine (Muscadet or Sancerre would be lovely)

3 large tomatoes, thinly sliced

2 medium white onions, thinly sliced

2 lemons, thinly sliced and pips removed

2 fresh bay leaves

2 sprigs of fresh thyme

1 sprig of fresh rosemary, snapped in two

2 cloves

3 tbsp olive oil

salt and freshly ground black pepper

2 tbsp chopped fresh parsley

crusty bread, to serve

For the aioli:

3 garlic cloves, finely chopped

2 egg yolks

pinch of saffron threads

2 tbsp milk

250ml / 9fl oz / 1 cup extra virgin olive oil

sea salt

Chef's tip:
Whenever possible preheat your oven for at least 30 minutes before using. I also pre-heat about 10°C / 50°F above the cooking temperature. By the time you open the door, load the oven and close the door, you'll have lost those extra few degrees and be nearer the desired cooking temperature.

Preheat the oven to 190°C / 375°F / gas mark 5 for at least 30 minutes.

In a large ovenproof dish, lay fillets of cod, skin side up. Pour wine over and around fish. Shingle alternating tomato, onion and lemon slices over each fillet (at least two of each per fillet). Place bay leaves, thyme, rosemary and cloves in the liquid around the fillets. Bake, uncovered, for 15 minutes.

To make the aioli, place the finely chopped garlic cloves, yolks, a pinch of sea salt, saffron, milk and 2 tablespoons of the olive oil in a large jug or high-sided container. Blitz with a hand-held blender to mix. With blender running, slowly drizzle in the remaining olive oil until you get a smooth, mayonnaise-like sauce. Season to taste with sea salt.

Garnish the baked fish with parsley and serve on the table in the baking dish with aioli and crusty bread.

BUTTER-TOASTED QUINOA WITH PETITS POIS

Serves 6

500g / 1lb 2oz red or white quinoa
100g / 3½oz / ½ cup butter, melted
200g / 7oz / 1½ cups petits pois (baby peas)
sea salt to taste

Preheat the oven to 190°C / 375°F / gas mark 5.

Toast the dry quinoa on a baking tray for 5–7 minutes, until golden, if using white quinoa – it should be a shade darker if using red.

While quinoa is toasting, bring a large pot of salted water to a boil. Add toasted quinoa and boil for 7–9 minutes (a bit longer for red) until just tender.

Add petits pois (if using frozen baby peas, run under cool water in a colander for a few moments first) and cook for an additional 1 minute. Drain well and toss well but gently with melted butter. Season to taste. Can be moulded in buttered ramekins and turned out for serving, if you like.

Chef's tip:
If using quinoa but not toasting the grains, be sure to rinse very well. There is a coating on the grains which, if not rinsed or toasted, will leave an unpleasant taste no matter how you cook or dress it.

BAKED LEMON TART

Serves 6–8

For the pastry:

2 eggs

80g / 2¾oz / ⅔ cup icing (powdered) sugar

100g / 3½oz / ½ cup butter, very soft

300g / 10½oz / 2 cups plain (all-purpose) flour

For the filling:

5 eggs

5 egg yolks

200g / 7oz / 1 cup caster (superfine) sugar

2 drops of vanilla extract

250ml / 9fl oz / 1 cup double (heavy) cream

4 lemons, zest of 1 and juice of all 4, seeds and pulp removed

To make the pastry, in a large bowl with a sturdy whisk, beat the eggs with icing sugar for 1 minute. Add softened butter and whisk to a single consistency. Add flour and work briefly until combined. Turn out onto a lightly floured surface and knead a few times to form a dough. Wrap in cling film and refrigerate for 30 minutes.

Preheat the oven to 180°C / 350°F / gas mark 4.

Roll out on a lightly floured surface and press into a tart pan. Prick the bottom several times with a fork. Bake until a light golden colour, about 20 minutes.

To make the filling, while the dough is baking, in a large bowl whisk the whole eggs and egg yolks with caster sugar and vanilla for 1 minute. Add cream, the zest of one lemon and the juice of all four lemons. Whisk well. Pour into the still-hot par-baked tart shell.

Continue to bake for 10–15 minutes, giving it a quarter turn four times during the baking time, until filling is set but still slightly wobbly. Cool to room temperature.

Chef's tip:
During the winter months, you may be able to find Meyer lemons at your greengrocer. They are a particular treat – a bit sweeter than ordinary lemons. Try this dish with Meyer lemons and you'll have a new favourite.

Scallop parcels in
martini sauce
(see page 93)

MAJA BEAUJOUAN

The Little Cheese Shop

FROM GERMANY WITH LOVE

*In front of her shop on Gray's Lane, Maja takes a
break to plan a meal just like her mother made*

FOR THOSE WHO HAVE VISITED Maja Beaujouan's Little Cheese Shop in Dingle, it won't be a surprise to learn how many awards and accolades the Black Forest-born German native has accumulated. If you have not yet had the pleasure, simply know that among her many achievements was being named the first-ever Grand Champion of the Blas na hÉireann (Taste of Ireland) Awards.

Growing up in a scratch kitchen and knowing the physical and emotional benefits of real food cooked with knowledge and love, Maja is dedicated to carrying on that tradition and passing it along to her four children.

She began cooking 'professionally' when she lived on a communal organic farm. With a young daughter on her hip, it made more sense for Maja to work in the kitchen rather than in the fields. It was also in these farmhouse kitchens that Maja developed her passion for using seasonal ingredients when available, preserving surplus for the lean times and creating wholesome foods that appealed to a broad range of tastes and appetites. It's also where she first learned how to make cheese.

As her daughter grew, Maja began working in the farm's dairy, first milking cows, then helping the cheesemaker, who became a dear friend. After a good few months she was asked to take over the position while the cheesemaker was away for a short holiday. After four years, her mentor felt she had taught Maja all that she could and suggested that she take an apprenticeship with the same master she had learned from in the Swiss Alps, where Maja duly spent the next several years working and training.

Realising that she was now a fully qualified maker of artisan cheeses and with a child ready for school, she decided to follow her parents, who had moved to the Dingle Peninsula two years earlier to set up shop in Stradbally, and set up her home and cheese-making kitchen in the small Kilcummin farm her parents had purchased as an eventual retirement property. The year was 1997 and artisan cheese and west Kerry were not synonymous – not yet.

There was something Old World about the way that things were still done in Dingle that Maja hadn't found in her homeland. Here, she found that young people and old still lived and talked and laughed and worked together. There was no such thing as a quick trip to the shop because you met your neighbours and discussed the important and the mundane right there on the footpath. The local pubs and markets were the breeding grounds for ideas and the places where the real work got done. She liked that way of life for herself and felt it would be a perfect setting to raise her child in.

Imagine the reaction of the farmers from below the hill when a young German woman walked up to their gate and asked to purchase raw milk to make into cheese, which she would produce by hand, using love and natural biologics rather than institutional methods and industrial ingredients. The response wasn't what you might think. Dingle being a small village, everyone already knew her intentions. Word of a vanload of cheese-making equipment being hauled up a muddy farm boreen gets around quickly.

Maja felt supported by her local community from the start and she still feels that way. The first customers to sample Maja's cheeses were patrons of Cork city's English Market, where On the Pig's Back, which was still small at the time, had set up a stall and were delighted to have a quality Irish cheese to sell alongside their offerings from the continent.

Her reputation quickly spread and in short order Maja became a founding stallholder of the Dingle farmers' market. She soon found herself selling out of her cheeses at the farmers' market in Tralee too, where she met an interesting Frenchman who was making charcuterie, foraging seaweeds and, importantly, had a refrigerated van.

Those awards started arriving, and so did the press. Maja needed a way to get her produce to a larger audience further afield, but she couldn't travel without a more reliable mode of transport. Olivier Beaujouan not only had just such a vehicle, but was also expanding his market through those same large fairs and festivals around Ireland. Long trips in the grey hours of the early mornings and back home again late in the evenings brought the two closer together and they fell in love and eventually married.

Maja opened the Little Cheese Shop in 2010, the same year that the food festival began and after the couple's third child was in school. She and her family have been an important part of the artisan food scene in Dingle from the beginning and continue to move the bar higher and higher.

I love recipes that call for sliding a simmering pot into a low oven for hours, and this menu uses one of the best. It's something you can set to cooking while you go hike the mountains behind the cottage or take the dogs to the beach. When you return, you'll be greeted by aromas that will embrace you like a grandmother's hug. You'll love Maja's garlic potato mousse for this menu, but Paul McPhillemy's black pepper spätzle (page 145) or Ondřej Hasík's boiled Czech dumplings (page 210) would go nicely as well.

FROM MOTHER'S TABLE

starter
Green salad with apples, avocado and lemon mustard dressing

main
Mami's beef goulash

side
Garlic potato mousse

dessert
Mousse au chocolat

cocktail suggestion
Black Velvet (page 251)

wine suggestion
Zweigelt from Austria

GREEN SALAD WITH APPLES, AVOCADO AND LEMON MUSTARD DRESSING

Serves 6

1 head of cos (romaine) lettuce, torn and washed
3 sweet apples, skin on, cored, halved and thinly sliced
3 avocados, halved and sliced (5–6 slices per half)

For the dressing:
1 tbsp spicy mustard
½ lemon, juiced, pulp and pips removed
1½ tbsp rice syrup
60ml / 2fl oz / ¼ cup olive oil
salt and freshly ground black pepper

In a small bowl mix the mustard, lemon juice, rice syrup and a pinch each of salt and pepper until all are nicely combined. Whisk while slowly adding the olive oil. You will end up with a mayonnaise-like consistency. Season to taste.

In a large bowl, toss lettuce and apple slices with half of the dressing. Season with salt and pepper.

Divide salad between six plates. Top with a shingle of the avocado and place a small dollop of remaining dressing on top.

Chef's tip:
Rice syrup (made with brown rice) is derived from brown rice the same way corn syrup is made from corn. There is a rich, malty flavour to rice syrup that is unlike any other sweetener so any substitution will change the taste of this dressing.

MAMI'S BEEF GOULASH

Serves 6–8

600g / 1lb 5oz medium-lean beef or buffalo meat, cut into 3cm / 1¼in pieces
3 tbsp rice flour or buckwheat flour
1–2 tbsp coconut oil, plus extra if needed
2 medium onions, sliced
150g / 5¼oz smoked lardons or bacon, cut into small pieces
2 garlic cloves, sliced
1 medium carrot, halved lengthwise and cut into 1cm / ½in pieces
1 red bell pepper, diced
1 small hot red pepper, seeded, ribbed and finely chopped (optional)
1 tsp paprika
120g / 4¼oz tomato purée (paste)
200ml / 7fl oz / ¾ cup + 4 tsp red wine
1.5 litres / 2¾ pints / 6 cups beef stock
salt and freshly ground black pepper

Preheat the oven to 130°C / 270°F / gas mark ½. In a medium bowl toss meat with the flour.

In a large, ovenproof casserole (Dutch oven) over medium–high heat add 1–2 tablespoons of coconut oil and heat to a shimmer. Add meat, one handful per batch – so as not to crowd the pan – and brown on all sides. Place each batch of browned meat in a colander set over a bowl to collect juices. Brown all meat, adding more oil as needed.

Pour off all but 1 tablespoon of the oil and add the onion and smoked lardons to the casserole. Reduce heat to medium and cook, stirring from time to time, until the onion starts to brown. Add the garlic, carrot, red bell pepper, hot red pepper, if using, and paprika. Cook for another 4 minutes.

Add the meat and the tomato purée and stir well. Adjust heat if needed so as not to burn and cook for an additional 3–4 minutes.

Deglaze with wine, scraping up the brown bits from the bottom. Bring to a simmer and reduce for 2–3 minutes. Add stock, reserved meat juices and a little salt and pepper.

Cover and cook in oven for about 2–2½ hours, until meat is very tender. Correct the seasoning and serve with potato mousse.

GARLIC POTATO MOUSSE

Serves 6

1.5kg / 3¼lb potatoes, peeled and quartered

500g / 1lb 2oz carrots, peeled and cut into 5mm / ¼in slices

2 garlic cloves, peeled

4 fresh bay leaves

1.4 litres / 2½ pints / 5⅔ cups milk

1.4 litres / 2½ pints / 5⅔ cups water

6 tbsp olive oil

salt and freshly ground black pepper

In a large pot cover the potatoes, carrots, garlic and bay leaves with milk and water and 2 teaspoons of salt. Set over high heat, bring nearly to a boil and reduce the heat to medium and a gentle simmer for about 15 minutes, until the potatoes are tender.

Drain in a colander but keep 400ml / 14fl oz / 1⅔ cups of the cooking liquid. Let vegetables dry a bit, but discard the bay leaves. Mash the potato, garlic and carrot mix either by hand or, even better, through a food mill. Stir in olive oil and thin as desired with cooking liquid. Correct the seasoning.

MOUSSE AU CHOCOLAT

Serves 6

200g / 7oz dark chocolate (70–80% cocoa solids)

5 eggs, separated

250g / 9oz / 1¼ cups caster (superfine) sugar

500ml / 18fl oz / 2 cups cream

pinch of salt

2–3 tbsp pear or cherry brandy

1 punnet (basket) of fresh berries, washed and dried

cocoa powder, to decorate

Break chocolate into large pieces and place in a heavy-bottomed pot.

In a clean bowl, whisk egg yolks with one third of the sugar until pale and fluffy. In a separate bowl, whisk the egg white with half of the rest of the sugar to stiff peaks. In a third bowl, whip cream with the remaining sugar to stiff peaks.

Boil water in a kettle. When hot, pour over the chocolate. Wait 3 minutes, pour off the water and blot pot dry with a piece of kitchen paper (paper towel) so no water is left in the pot. Stir the chocolate. Fold melted chocolate into egg yolk mixture to incorporate completely.

Quickly whisk the whipped cream into chocolate and egg mixture, then add the salt and brandy. Carefully fold the egg whites into the mousse so there are no streaks.

Pour mousse into a clean bowl, cover with cling film, pressing it onto the surface of the mousse so no skin forms, and chill for at least 6 hours or overnight.

To serve, place a serving spoon into a container of very hot water. Scoop the mousse with hot spoon and place in serving dishes with berries and a dusting of cocoa powder.

OLIVIER BEAUJOUAN

On the Wild Side

A LOVABLE RAKE

With a broad smile and a strong accent, Olivier ('Olly' to his friends) offers up tempting creations at farmers' markets all around Munster

OLIVIER BEAUJOUAN is one of those loveable rakes you hear about in the artisan food business: a massive talent with a mischievous glint in his eye. You never know what direction a conversation with Olivier will take you. It's a long road from Tours in France's Loire Valley to the Dingle Peninsula, even in a straight line, and Olivier did not take the direct route. Growing up one generation removed from the family farm, Olivier inherited his father's love of the land and livestock, and of pigs in particular. It was for this reason that his career path began with a butchery and charcuterie apprenticeship under three different masters in the city of Tours.

Moving around throughout France, Italy and Spain, from the mountains to the sea, working in shops and cafés for half a decade, he expanded his understanding of his craft to include fish, wild game and sea vegetables. He always moved with the season, with the crowds and with the next opportunity in mind. Then, without a word of English, he set off for a job he'd heard about in Glasgow, Scotland.

Although he got on well enough he never felt quite comfortable in Glasgow, so he took a ferry to Belfast and the next day a train to Dublin. The year was 1994. The date was 17 March: Paddy's Day!

Finding little call for the skills of a salumist, Olivier found work in some of the best Dublin kitchens run by French chefs. Not having come up under the strict discipline of the French brigade system, he bristled under the yoke of domineering chefs and jealous demi chefs. So when he discovered the farmers' market that was up and running in the Temple Bar district, he knew he'd found his ticket out of the kitchens and back into his passion for charcuterie.

During this time Olivier also picked up a copy of what he calls 'the bible', *Food for Free* by Richard Mabey, and he became known for the quality of the wild foods he would bring to restaurants. This also gave him access to commercial kitchen space from which to develop his now signature pâté using foraged ingredients with local organic meats and fish. While selling in the farmers' market in Tralee, he found permanent space for a kitchen from which to supply customers at five or six markets throughout Munster each week.

Local tastes have changed a lot since Olivier first tried to sell his handcrafted products back when all that most Irish people knew of charcuterie were ham and bacon. Sure, the occasional fisherman's wife might have made a smoked mackerel pâté, but smoked goose salami, pickled seaweed salad and dry-cured pig's jowl were not on many families' shopping lists. Today, though, people seek out On the Wild Side's award-winning products. I for one always have at least three kinds of Olivier's salamis hanging in my kitchen.

While products with many of the same names can be found in multinational supermarkets across Ireland today, Olivier believes in using quality products from small Irish farmers who feel the same way about food that he does.

Ireland's tastes continue to change. You'd be hard pressed to find anyone in the business who would argue with the fact that this playful Frenchman was part of that change. Perhaps tastes have changed enough, even, to have a go at this French classic. I do hope I get invited to this party ...

Outside of Lyon in France, it may be difficult to get your hands on the head of a calf for tête de veau. Even if you can find one, many reading this book would scoff at the very idea of cooking such a dish. Just remember that non-prime cuts of meat always have the most flavour – it just takes time and talent to coax them onto the plate. There are some who would travel thousands of miles and pay a high price to have dishes like this prepared for and served to them. A simple side of boiled potatoes is traditional with tête de veau, but Eric Maillard's sauté potatoes (page 203) or Fernando Lovisetto's polenta (page 164) would also make wonderful accompaniments. I've made the cocktail particularly strong for those faint of heart ...

AN ADVENTUROUS SUNDAY LUNCH

starter
Lamb's lettuce and beetroot salad with chive vinaigrette

main
Tête de veau with sauce gribiche

dessert
Mother's rhubarb tart

cocktail suggestion
Dingle Vesper Martini (page 255)

wine suggestion
Côtes du Jura Rouge

LAMB'S LETTUCE AND BEETROOT SALAD WITH CHIVE VINAIGRETTE

Serves 6

3 large beetroot, washed
200g / 7oz lamb's lettuce, washed
and dried

For the dressing:
2 tbsp cider vinegar
1 tbsp Dijon mustard
6 tbsp extra virgin olive oil
1 bunch of fresh chives, snipped
sea salt

In a large pot of salted water, bring beetroot to a boil, reduce to simmer and cook until just tender. Remove from heat and let cool in the cooking liquid – overnight is fine.

To make the dressing, whisk vinegar and mustard together. Continue to whisk while you drizzle in olive oil. Fold in chives and season with salt.

To assemble the salad, pat dry the cooled beetroot, peel and thinly slice. Arrange beetroot slices around the edges of six serving plates.

In a large bowl, toss lamb's lettuce with dressing and place in the centre of the plates.

Chef's tip:
Lamb's lettuce is sometimes known as mâche or corn salad (because it is actually something of a weed found growing among cereal crops). The leaves are small – about the size and shape of a lamb's tongue, hence the name – and slightly waxy but they have a tender texture and tang on the palate that is quite pleasant and they're worth seeking out.

TÊTE DE VEAU WITH SAUCE GRIBICHE

Serves 6 with leftovers

1 veal head – have your butcher bone, roll and tie it and make sure they leave the tongue in

4 celery stalks

2 leeks, split lengthwise

2 carrots, peeled and split lengthwise

2 onions, peeled and halved

4 fresh bay leaves

4 cloves

1 bunch of fresh parsley

4 sprigs of fresh thyme

12 black peppercorns

2 tbsp sea salt

500ml / 18fl oz / 2 cups white wine

crusty bread, to serve

For the sauce gribiche:

2 egg yolks

1 tbsp Dijon mustard

100ml / 3½fl oz / ⅓ cup + 4 tsp cider vinegar

400ml / 14fl oz / 1⅔ cups sunflower oil

1 hardboiled egg, peeled and diced

5 cornichons (French tarragon-flavoured pickled gherkins available in speciality markets), finely chopped

15 capers, finely chopped

salt and freshly ground black pepper

Place rolled veal head into a very large pot. Add all the vegetables save the onion halves. Spike each onion half with a bay leaf and clove. Add these onions and the other herbs, salt and peppercorns to the pot. Add wine and enough cold water to cover by 10cm / 4in.

Bring to a simmer over medium–high heat, then reduce to medium–low and poach the veal for 6 hours. Allow to cool in the cooking liquid for about 1 hour.

To make the sauce gribiche, place yolks, mustard and vinegar in a medium-sized bowl and whisk together.

While whisking, slowly drizzle in the oil. You will have a mayonnaise-like consistency when finished. Fold in chopped egg, cornichons and capers. Season with salt and pepper to taste.

Slice the veal and serve with sauce gribiche and crusty bread (chef also likes to serve the leeks and carrot from the cooking liquid as well).

MOTHER'S RHUBARB TART

Serves 6–8

For the pastry:

2 eggs

80g / 2¾oz / ⅔ cup icing (powdered) sugar

100g / 3½oz / ½ cup butter, very soft

300g / 10½oz / 2 cups plain (all-purpose) flour

For the filling:

850g / 1lb 14oz rhubarb

2 tbsp sugar

50g / 1¾oz / ⅓ cup plain (all-purpose) flour

80ml / 3fl oz / ⅓ cup cream

3 eggs

70g / 2½oz / ⅓ cup brown sugar

icing (powdered) sugar, for dusting

200ml / 7fl oz / ¾ cup + 4 tsp cream, whipped, to serve

DAY 1

Peel, wash and dry rhubarb, cut into 2–3cm / ¾–1¼in cubes. Toss them in some sugar and leave them overnight.

To make the pastry, in a large bowl using a sturdy whisk, beat two whole eggs with icing sugar for 1 minute. Add softened butter and whisk to a single consistency. Add flour and work briefly until combined. Turn out onto a lightly floured surface and knead a few times to form a dough. Wrap in cling film and refrigerate overnight.

DAY 2

Preheat the oven to 180°C / 350°F / gas mark 4.

Drain the rhubarb and discard the bitter juice.

Roll out pastry dough and mould into a 23cm / 9in tart tin with a removable bottom. Add the rhubarb cubes and distribute evenly.

In a bowl, whisk the flour, cream, eggs and brown sugar together.

Pour the egg mixture over the rhubarb and bake for 35 minutes. Cool for at least 30 minutes. Dust with icing sugar and serve with whipped cream.

Chef's tip:
Where I grew up you'd almost never see a rhubarb dessert that wasn't paired with strawberries. This use of the vegetable (yes, rhubarb is actually a vegetable), sweetened and baked in rustic custard is a wonderful way to use rhubarb alone.

MARK MURPHY

Dingle Cookery School

MARKET FRESH

Wherever the food is fresh, local, and artisanal,
you'll find local food hero Mark Murphy

AS RECENTLY AS THE EARLY NOUGHTIES, the extent of Mark Murphy's menu choices and cooking abilities ranged from instant noodles to whatever grot in the pot his backpacking budget and hostel kitchens might provide. After studies in sports management, the former rugby player headed off with his rucksack and trekked around Europe, Australia, New Zealand and South-East Asia, even making it as far as Alaska and the Northwest Territories of Canada.

While Mark had no real interest in cooking food when he set off from Carlow, he loved to eat and the vastness and colour of local markets grabbed the young man's attention. He began to wish that his knowledge and ability extended beyond a simple attraction to food and that he understood it better. At the same time, he was also starting to realise the power of food to gather a group of diverse people together around a communal table.

He began by sorting out eight or ten dishes that he could master – dishes that could be put together on a budget, please a small crowd and that would let him experience these local markets in a way he'd not yet been able to. This budding passion is what finally brought him back to Ireland, where he enrolled in the Galway-Mayo Institute of Technology's culinary arts programme. A few months before his classes were due to begin, he came down to Dingle for an afternoon with a friend and his plans were turned on their head. He eventually changed his college plans from Galway to Tralee, rented an apartment in Dingle, worked in a local Italian restaurant, commuted to classes via the Conor Pass and began a long love affair with Dingle.

As he studied and attended his industry placements in some of the finest restaurants and guesthouses in the country, Mark began to realise that it was not just cooking, but the educational process of cooking, that he really loved. He completed his master's degree in new food products and culinary innovation in order to

better his chances at nabbing one of the elusive teaching positions at an institute of technology. During his advanced studies, the importance of local markets, including farmers' markets, came into focus for Mark.

His love for the peninsula deepened as he helped expand the Dingle farmers' market and took on the adventure of developing the relationship between the

Dingle Food Festival and high-quality market stallholders from around the country – a crowd favourite every year.

Mark was part of the trio who brought the Dingle Cookery School to the town and he continues to grow and expand the classes, both professional courses and hobby classes that range all over the cookery spectrum. His efforts earned him the Munster Local Food Hero award from the Restaurant Association of Ireland in 2016.

When time permits, Mark still travels to visit farmers' markets and food festivals around Ireland to see what's happening in all corners of the country as the culture of high-quality local produce expands in large cities and small towns. But he still finds his emotions stirred every time he crests the hill at the viewing point at the top of the pass on his way home.

The food, music, art and culture, the scenery and the outdoor activities that attract vast numbers of tourists every year are some of the things that keep the travelling heart of Mark Murphy from leaving. It's a special place. Everyone who comes here to visit knows this. It's even more special for those of us who get to call Dingle our home. Mark Murphy came to Dingle for an afternoon in 2004, and while his cooking career took him away for a while, he never really left.

Between his teaching gigs, demonstrations, consulting and community involvement, you might think that Mark wouldn't have time for such an elaborate dinner party. But you'll see a chef's sensibility in this menu when you consider how much can be made ahead of time – over several days, even – and simply heated and finished as your guests arrive. A half hour of preparation here and there throughout the week and your menu will be ready for your weekend soirée. If one of your guests doesn't like turnip (though I must say I love their addition in Mark's dish), substitute Niall Ó Conchúir's potato gratin (page 175) and everyone will be happy.

AUTUMN DINNER FROM THE MARKETS

starter
Crispy goat's cheese salad with orange and cumin yogurt dressing

main
Braised short ribs of beef

side
Potato and turnip gratin

dessert
Chocolate fondant with coffee and chocolate crumble

cocktail suggestion
Pink Gin (page 260)

wine suggestion
Barolo

CRISPY GOAT'S CHEESE SALAD WITH ORANGE AND CUMIN YOGURT DRESSING

Serves 6

3–4 carrots, peeled and cut into even-sized lengths

3–4 beetroot, cut into even-sized wedges

2 garlic cloves, finely chopped

½ tsp cumin seeds

1 tsp coriander seeds

1 orange, zested and halved

1 large red bell pepper, cut into long strips

salt and freshly ground black pepper

selection of hearty salad leaves, such as radicchio, mustard leaves and mizuna

For the dressing:

60ml / 2fl oz / ¼ cup natural yogurt

zest from the orange

1 tbsp lemon juice

salt and freshly ground black pepper

For the crispy goat's cheese

100g / 3½oz / 1⅓ cups panko Japanese-style breadcrumbs

2 tsp thyme leaves, picked and very finely chopped

salt and freshly ground black pepper

2 eggs, beaten

100g / 3½oz / ⅔ cup plain (all-purpose) flour

150g / 5¼oz goat's cheese, cut into six portions

oil, for frying

Preheat the oven to 180°C / 350°F / gas mark 4. Place a baking tray in the oven to heat up too. Bring two large pots of salted water to a boil. Add the carrots to one pot and the beetroot to the other. Return to a boil, reduce to a simmer and cook them for about 5 minutes. Strain the vegetables and place on the hot baking tray. Add the garlic, cumin, coriander and the juice of half an orange to the hot vegetables, season and roast for 15 minutes.

Drain the liquid from the tray into a bowl with juice of remaining orange half. Add the strips of red pepper to the tray and continue to roast for 5–10 more minutes.

Wash and dry salad greens. Set aside.

To make the dressing, place yogurt in a small bowl, stir in some of the juices from the baking tray (1–2 tablespoons should be plenty), then add orange zest followed by the lemon juice. Season with some salt and pepper.

To make the crispy goat's cheese, season the breadcrumbs with thyme, salt and pepper. Put the flour, beaten egg and breadcrumbs in three separate bowls and keep them in that order.

Dip each piece of goat's cheese in the flour and then in the egg. Use the other hand to take it from the egg and add it to the breadcrumbs, pressing crumbs into the cheese to coat well. Repeat this process with the rest of the goat's cheese. Keep this aside until just before serving.

To serve, heat a large sauté pan over medium–high heat, add enough oil to coat the bottom of the pan. Carefully add the breaded goat's cheese and cook for about 2 minutes before turning it over. The breadcrumbs should be a golden colour.

Place the salad leaves in a large bowl, mix in just enough dressing and toss well. Divide the salad between six bowls.

In the same mixing bowl, add roasted vegetables and toss in a little dressing. Arrange in bowls with salad, place the warm goat's cheese on top of the salad and serve immediately.

BRAISED SHORT RIBS OF BEEF

Serves 6

6 beef short ribs

dash of olive oil

1 onion, cut into large dice

1 large head of garlic, cut in half horizontally

1 bunch of fresh thyme

1 bunch of fresh rosemary

1 tbsp tomato purée (paste)

500ml / 18fl oz / 2 cups red wine (I like Barolo in this dish, particularly if you're serving it with your meal)

500ml / 18fl oz / 2 cups beef stock

salt and freshly ground black pepper

3 tbsp finely chopped fresh flat-leaf parsley

Preheat the oven to 150°C / 300°F / gas mark 2. Place a roasting tin in the oven for 30 minutes to heat up.

Season the short ribs with plenty of salt and pepper, place hot roasting tin over medium–high heat (you may need two burners to do this) and immediately add the ribs. Brown for about 10 minutes on each side. Once they have been browned remove them from the tin while you prepare the rest of the ingredients.

Wipe out any excess oil from the tin. Add the diced onion, garlic (cut side down) and herbs. Let them brown for 2–3 minutes. When they have taken on a nice brown colour add the tomato purée, stirring for a minute or two.

Add the wine to deglaze the pan, scraping the brown bits from the tray. Bring the wine to a boil and cook for about 10 minutes, until it is reduced by half. Add the stock. Return the ribs to the tray.

Cover the tray with foil and place in the oven. Check it after about 2 hours to make sure there is liquid in the tray; if not, add a little water or stock. Continue cooking for 4–5 hours in total, until the meat comes easily off the bone.

Carefully remove the ribs to a warm serving plate and keep them warm while you finish the sauce.

Put a strainer over a pot and pour the contents of the tray into the strainer. Using a ladle press all the juice from the vegetables. Skim off the fat. Place the pot over a medium heat and cook the liquid for about 10 minutes. The liquid will thicken to give you a rich, syrupy sauce. Season with salt and pepper and pour the sauce over the ribs and garnish with chopped parsley.

POTATO AND TURNIP GRATIN

Serves 6–8

500ml / 18fl oz / 2 cups cream

1 tsp thyme leaves, picked

4 garlic cloves, crushed

1 large turnip, sliced finely and stamped into discs

4–6 potatoes, peeled and sliced

100g / 3½oz / 1 cup grated Coolattin cheese (or your favourite mature Cheddar cheese)

20g / ¾oz / 4 tsp butter, cubed

100g / 3½oz / ¾ cup fresh breadcrumbs cooked in 1 tbsp butter

salt and freshly ground black pepper

Preheat the oven to 180°C / 350°F / gas mark 4.

In a small saucepan over medium heat add cream, thyme, garlic and a little salt and pepper. Heat for 5 minutes. Turn off and leave to steep for 20 minutes. Strain the liquid, discarding solids. Set aside.

In a large ovenproof dish, layer half of the potato and turnip slices. Top with half of the cream and season with salt and pepper. Repeat with remaining potato, turnip and cream. Season.

Cover the dish with foil and bake for 40 minutes. Remove the foil and scatter over the cheese, butter and breadcrumbs. Reduce heat to 150ºC / 300°F / gas mark 2 and continue to bake for about 30 minutes, until golden brown and bubbly.

CHOCOLATE FONDANT WITH COFFEE AND CHOCOLATE CRUMBLE

Makes 9 fondants

For the crumble:
50g / 1¾oz / ¼ cup caster sugar
50g / 1¾oz / ½ cup ground almonds
40g / 1½oz / ¼ cup plain (all-purpose) flour
10g / ¼oz / 2 tbsp cocoa powder
25g / ¾oz / ⅓ cup ground coffee
30g / 1oz / 2 tbsp butter, melted

For the fondant:
45g / 1½oz / 3 tbsp butter, melted
50g / 1¾oz / ½ cup cocoa powder
200g / 7oz dark chocolate (70–80% cocoa solids), chopped into small pieces
200g / 7oz butter, cut into small pieces
4 eggs
4 egg yolks
200g / 7oz / 1 cup golden caster sugar (see Chef's Tip on page 12)
200g / 7oz / 1⅓ cups plain (all-purpose) flour

Preheat the oven to 180°C / 350°F / gas mark 4.

To make the crumble, toss dry ingredients together in a large mixing bowl, then fold in butter. Spread evenly on a baking tray and bake for 15–20 minutes. Allow to cool and then pulse in a food processor to create a fine crumb. Set aside.

To make the fondants, using upward strokes, heavily brush the melted butter all over the inside of 9 x 150ml / 5¼fl oz / ⅔ cup pudding moulds or large ramekins. Place moulds into the refrigerator. Once the moulds are chilled, brush more melted butter over the top of the set, chilled butter. Add a teaspoon of cocoa powder to the moulds. Tip and tap the moulds to cover the butter completely with cocoa powder. Tap out any excess cocoa.

Place a bowl with chocolate and butter pieces over a pan of barely simmering water and stir to melt. Remove bowl from heat and stir until smooth. Leave to cool for about 10 minutes.

In another bowl whisk the eggs and yolks together with the sugar to ribbon stage – thick and pale and the whisk leaves a trail. Sift the flour into the eggs and whisk together.

Pour the melted chocolate into the egg mixture in thirds, whisking well between each addition, until all the chocolate has been added and the mixture is completely combined into a loose cake batter.

Divide the batter between the moulds. Chill for a minimum of 20 minutes or up to 24 hours. (These can now be frozen for up to one month and cooked from frozen.)

Preheat the oven to 200°C / 400°F / gas mark 6.

Place the fondants on a baking tray and bake in the oven for 10–12 minutes, until the tops have formed a crust and they are just starting to come away from the sides of the moulds. Remove from the oven and then let them sit for 1 minute before turning out.

Loosen the fondants by moving the tops very gently so they come away from the sides, easing them out of the moulds. Tip each fondant slightly onto your hand so you know that it has come away, then tip back into the mould, put a plate on top and turn it over. Decorate the plate with a dusting of coffee crumble.

ANNE LONG

The Dingle Bay Hotel

BORN TO COOK

On the street where she was born and has worked her entire life,
it doesn't get much more 'Dingle' than Anne Long

NOT ALL THE CHEFS in Dingle come from other places or travelled the world in search of their cooking styles: Anne Long never even left the home she was born in.

Born in the back bedroom of a house on Strand Street that also housed a grocer's shop, a fishmonger's shop, a bar and a shed out the back where fish were salted and smoked for export, Anne grew up with food businesses all around her. Her first jobs included cutting the rinds from rashers of bacon and odd jobs for local publicans when she was in her teens. It seems that this Dingle native was born to cook.

Though the premises that was once Anne Long's childhood abode has been remodelled, knocked down and rebuilt at least four times since she was born and even though she now resides further 'Back West', the ground where the Dingle Bay Hotel and Paudie's Bar stand is the place she most thinks of as home.

Her first go at serving food from the place came in the form of a kind of delicatessen counter where the fishmonger's shop had once been. The offerings of cold boiled lobsters, crab cocktails, fish chowder and a few similar items proved so popular with locals and tourists that, as Anne says, 'a few tables just showed up one day' and off they went.

The success of the shop as well as Anne's innate talent led the family to knock the building and construct a small B&B with six guestrooms adjacent to the family's living quarters along with a purpose-built new bar and restaurant. Anne was at the

helm of the kitchen with nothing but a two-week course at Cork's famed Ballymaloe Cookery School under her belt, and customers loved the place almost as much as their chef did.

Anne's food was fresh, there's no doubt about that. Lobsters were caught by her husband and landed twice a day. Fish came when the day boats landed them just a few hundred yards from the Longs' front door. Meat came from a local abattoir and was hand cut to order. She pushed her clientele in the early days by adding the influences of other cuisines to her dishes, but she soon learned that people wanted simply prepared, unadulterated foods, so that's what Anne gave them and they loved it.

With the niche of a harbour-side hotel unfilled in the town and the Celtic Tiger roaring its head off, the family decided once again to scrape the building to its foundation and built a 24-bedroom hotel with banqueting facilities and a busy public house.

Anne lost her beloved restaurant in the redesign, but she hasn't stopped cooking. Paudie's Bar is one of the busiest places for lunch during the season. Though customers will often ask for dishes that had been on Longs' menu or even on the opening menu for Paudie's Bar, Anne has tried to keep up with changing food fashions. Still, the traditional Irish favourites are the main draw and it's the kind of food that she still loves to cook, which she does for twelve to fifteen hours, three meals a day, during the busy seasons.

It's hard to separate Anne Long the chef of the Dingle Bay Hotel from Anne Long the person – she's been at it in this one location her whole life. She says she and her husband have had three families due to the gap in the ages of their children. Three incarnations of her kitchens, three families, and now Anne offers us a three-course menu that speaks of her rare few hours off during the summer. It's easy to prepare in advance so that you can enjoy the company of friends, relying on seasonal ingredients at their peak of perfection and in the company of those you hold dear. It's a taste of the Dingle Peninsula from someone who has spent her entire life here.

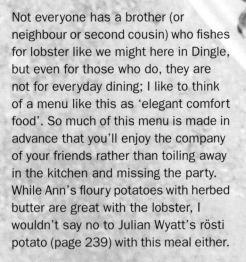

Not everyone has a brother (or neighbour or second cousin) who fishes for lobster like we might here in Dingle, but even for those who do, they are not for everyday dining; I like to think of a menu like this as 'elegant comfort food'. So much of this menu is made in advance that you'll enjoy the company of your friends rather than toiling away in the kitchen and missing the party. While Ann's floury potatoes with herbed butter are great with the lobster, I wouldn't say no to Julian Wyatt's rösti potato (page 239) with this meal either.

JULY IN ANNE'S GARDEN

starter
Butterhead lettuce soup

main
Anne's lobster thermidor

side
Baby gem salad with mustard seed dressing

Floury baked potatoes with fresh herb butter

dessert
Strawberry and raspberry pavlova

cocktail suggestion
French 75 (page 255)

wine suggestion
Meursault

Chef's tip:

The RSPCA's humane way to cook lobsters also creates a tender and juicy meat. In a large stockpot, cover the lobsters with lukewarm sea water (if you cannot use seawater, use 170g / 6oz fine sea salt for every 1.8 litres / 3¼ pints / ½ gallon of fresh water. It will be very salty, like the sea). Put the pot over low heat and slowly bring to a simmer. The lobsters will die at about 45°C / 113°F. By the time the water comes to a simmer, the lobsters will be ready for this dish.

For fully cooked lobsters: remove the lobsters and discard the seawater. Place 1 peeled, sliced carrot and 1 peeled, sliced onion into the pot with 2 cups of wine, 2 cups of water, 6 peppercorns and 2 bay leaves, bring to a boil, add lobsters and cover with a lid. Steam until the lobsters become bright orange (about 15 minutes for the first 500g / 1lb 2oz plus 10 more minutes for each additional 500g / 1lb 2 oz).

BUTTERHEAD LETTUCE SOUP

Serves 6

30g / 1oz / 2 tbsp butter

2 small onions, chopped

3 large potatoes, peeled and chopped

600ml / 1 pint / 2⅓ cups vegetable or chicken stock or water

2 heads of butterhead lettuce, washed and leaves torn

1 head of baby gem lettuce, washed and leaves torn

100ml / 3½fl oz / ⅓ cup + 4 tsp crème fraîche

2–3 sprigs fresh mint, chopped

salt and ground white pepper

In a heavy-bottomed pot over medium–low heat, melt butter. Add onions and a pinch of salt. Stir to coat with butter. Add potato, stir and cook until onions are translucent and potatoes begin to soften slightly – do not allow to colour. Add stock, increase heat to medium and bring to a simmer. Cook until potatoes are done.

Remove from heat and add lettuces. Stir to wilt, then blend with a hand-held blender until smooth. Season to taste.

Serve with a dollop of crème fraîche and a scattering of fresh mint.

Chef's tip:
Butterhead lettuce is also known as Boston lettuce in some markets. Baby gem is a small, compact lettuce that looks like a small head of romaine (cos). If you cannot find baby gem, hearts of romaine can be substituted, but don't use the outer, dark green leaves of the romaine. They'll be a bit too bitter for the soup.

ANNE'S LOBSTER THERMIDOR

Serves 6

3 x 675–700g / 1lb 8oz–1lb 9oz lobsters, boiled and cooled

30g / 1oz / 2 tbsp butter

4 shallots, diced

1 garlic clove, finely chopped

5 tomatoes, peeled, deseeded and finely diced

4 mushrooms, finely diced

1 celery stalk, finely diced

60ml / 2fl oz / ¼ cup brandy

180ml / 6fl oz / ¾ cup full-fat milk

180ml / 6fl oz / ¾ cup cream

2 tbsp tomato purée (paste)

2 pinches of cayenne pepper

3–4 heaped tsp cornflour (cornstarch) mixed with equal amount of water

200g / 7oz / 1⅔ cups fresh breadcrumbs toasted in butter with 1 tbsp chopped mixed fresh herbs

Preheat the oven to 180°C / 350°F / gas mark 4.

Cut lobsters in half. Take out tail meat. Clean out shell and discard stomach sack. Crack claws with the back of a chef's knife but keep intact. Arrange lobster bodies on a baking tray. Cut tail meat into large bite-sized pieces and set aside.

In a large sauté pan over medium–low heat, melt butter. Add shallots, garlic and tomatoes. Cook for about 4 minutes. Add mushrooms and celery, continue to cook for an additional 5–6 minutes, until celery begins to soften but still has some bite.

Increase heat to high. Add brandy, remove from heat and flambé. Return to heat and cook until flame goes out. Stir in milk, cream, tomato purée and cayenne pepper. Just before the sauce comes to a boil, add the cornflour mixture and whisk until sauce thickens.

Remove from heat and add lobster meat to sauce and carefully spoon lobster and sauce into the shells. Top with the buttery herb breadcrumbs and bake in the oven for 15 minutes.

BABY GEM SALAD WITH MUSTARD SEED DRESSING

Serves 6

6 heads of baby gem lettuce, washed, dried, quartered lengthwise and cored
6 plum tomatoes, cored and quartered
120g / 4¼oz roasted red peppers
6 spring onions (scallions), thinly sliced

For the mustard seed dressing:
1 tsp wholegrain mustard
1 tbsp honey
½ lemon, juiced
80ml / 3fl oz / ⅓ cup olive oil
80ml / 3fl oz / ⅓ cup rapeseed oil
salt and freshly ground black pepper

Arrange salad on chilled plates.

In a small bowl, combine mustard, honey and lemon juice. Combine oils and slowly whisk into the bowl. Season to taste, then drizzle the dressing over the salad.

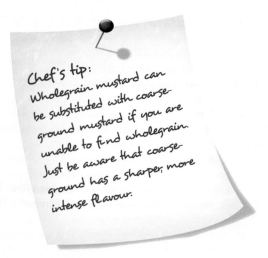

Chef's tip:
Wholegrain mustard can be substituted with coarse ground mustard if you are unable to find wholegrain. Just be aware that coarse ground has a sharper, more intense flavour.

134

FLOURY BAKED POTATOES WITH FRESH HERB BUTTER

Serves 6

6 Queen potatoes
60ml / 2fl oz / ¼ cup high-quality Irish rapeseed oil
2 tbsp Maldon flaky sea salt
170g / 6oz butter, softened
1 tbsp finely chopped fresh parsley
1 tbsp snipped fresh chives
1 tsp finely chopped fresh dill
salt and freshly ground black pepper

Preheat the oven to 200°C / 400°F / gas mark 6.

Wash and dry potatoes well, prick several times with a fork.

Pour some oil into your hands and rub over the potatoes. Place potatoes on a baking rack and sprinkle with Maldon salt, which should stick to the oil.

Bake for 1¼–1½ hours, depending on the size of the potatoes. When cooked, the potatoes should be golden brown and crisp on the outside and give a little when squeezed.

Meanwhile, mash soft butter with the back of a fork in a small bowl. Add herbs, salt and pepper to taste. Stir to mix completely. Keep in a cool, but not cold, place so that the butter stays soft.

Cut a zigzag slit in the top of each baked potato with a sharp knife, squeeze the sides to force the floury flesh a little way out of the top. Spoon some of the herb butter on the potato and serve.

Chef's tip:
If you cannot find Queen potatoes, Russets, Kerr's Pinks or Golden Wonders will work as well.

STRAWBERRY AND RASPBERRY PAVLOVA

Serves 6–8

350g / 12oz / 1¾ cups caster (superfine) sugar

2 tsp cornflour (cornstarch)

6 large egg whites

1 tsp white wine vinegar

1 drop of red food colouring

1 punnet (basket) of strawberries, washed, dried, hulled and sliced

1 punnet (basket) of raspberries, washed and dried

500ml / 18fl oz / 2 cups cream, whipped

organic pansy or violet flowers, to decorate

Preheat the oven to 110°C / 230°F / gas mark ¼. Adjust oven racks to upper middle and lower middle.

Using a 20cm / 8in cake pan as a guide, trace 2 x 20cm / 8in circles on each of two sheets of non-stick baking paper. Flip sheets over so that the pencil marks are on the bottom and lay the paper on two rimmed baking trays.

Combine caster sugar and cornflour in bowl.

In a large, clean mixing bowl, place egg whites and whip to soft billowy mounds. Slowly add the sugar and cornflour mixture as you continue to whip to soft peaks. Add vinegar and food colouring. Whip to stiff peaks.

Divide meringue evenly among all four circles on prepared trays and gently spread into even layers. Bake for 1¾ hours, switching and rotating the trays halfway through baking.

Turn off oven and allow meringues to cool in oven for at least 1 hour and up to overnight. Remove from oven and let cool to room temperature, about 15 minutes, if required.

To assemble, place one meringue round on large cake platter. Spread with one third of the whipped cream and scatter with one third of the berries. Repeat with remaining meringue rounds, whipped cream and berries, finishing with final meringue layer on top. Decorate with fresh edible flowers and serve immediately.

PAUL McPHILLEMY

Ashe's

GLOBALLY MENTORED

*With Seamus the Irish Wolfhound,
Paul McPhillemy takes a break by
the shores of Dingle Harbour*

PAUL MᴄPHILLEMY took an interest in food at an early age, when he would proffer suggestions to his mother as to how she might improve her offerings at the County Tyrone family's dinner table. One can only imagine an Ulster mother suffering the opinions of her son about the lamb and barley soup. When it came time for him to decide what to do after his secondary education, his mum suggested he head off to trade school and study to be a chef. Catering college in Derry led to his certification work at Omagh.

As a young man he bounced around jobs that allowed him to keep up with his outdoor hobbies with friends. He followed those mates over to London, where they'd secured work on building sites. In short order Paul found himself working in the two-man kitchen of a busy little French restaurant in Golders Green on the city's north side. It was here that he met his first mentor, who showed him the way a proper kitchen is set up for smooth operation and ingredients he hadn't worked with before. 'I didn't know half of what was going on in the kitchen, but the head chef was very patient with me and was a very good teacher,' Paul told me of his London experience.

After his first season the nineteen-year-old was a bit homesick, so he headed back to Strabane. With little cooking work available in the town, he went in on a fishing boat with his friends and spent three years hauling lobster pots and hand lining for mackerel, pollock and the like. It was good fun for a while, but the call back to the kitchen was growing louder and louder.

A short stay working at a hotel in Mullaghmore, County Sligo, introduced Paul to another mentor who saw his potential and sent him to Kilkea Castle to start his career in earnest. While there he worked under a chef who would go on to be a lecturer in the later years of his career. He was the kind of chef that everyone remembers as a firm but fair teacher who would offer you the opportunity to fix a mistake once, but wouldn't let you make it a second time.

After two years at Kilkea Castle, Paul had a bona fide lust for culinary knowledge and set off for a year-long exploration of Australia. He took a job in a St Regis hotel under a chef who sent him out on a series of short gigs after six months in the hotel. Picking up a day or two of work as he backpacked around the country, Paul was exposed to flavours and ingredients he'd never experienced in Ireland.

When he landed back in Ulster, his friends in the business told him that Dingle was a happening tourist town and needed chefs. He packed his knives, headed down the country and has never left.

Paul has seen a lot change since he moved to Dingle in 1998. He has worked from the far end of the peninsula and back to Dingle town. He has owned his own restaurant, has filled in for a season here and there, has got married and has two boys. He has seen the tastes of locals and tourists change, but not in the same way. 'The tourists from America aren't coming to Dingle for a curry,' he jokes, 'but the locals want to stretch a bit and love a bit of Asian flavour in their food once in a while.'

He also mentions that the 'fine' food of Ireland was stuck in the 1970s for so long that it seems like he's seen fifty years' worth of growth and taste change in just the past decade. He says that he cooks the kinds of food that he would want to eat when he goes out: 'rustic bar food' is what he calls it. Fancy, but accessible. Not uptight, but sophisticated. Highly flavoured, but not overwhelming.

As a young man Paul was mentored by adept men in quality kitchens. For two decades, Paul has been mentoring the palates of a generation of tourists and locals alike.

SURF AND TURF FROM NORTH AND SOUTH

starter
Crab dumpling with nước chấm dipping sauce

main
Braised pork belly with vanilla foam

sides
Black pepper spätzle

dessert
Ulster pineapple pie

cocktail suggestion
Singapore Gin Sling (page 262)

beverage suggestion
Dry to semi-dry cider from Normandy

Don't be put off when you see 'Day 1, Day 2 and Day 3' in the recipes for this menu. This is another menu where a little bit of work each day makes for an amazing dish that can be assembled in no time at all. As the pork belly is such a rich dish, Paul's light crab dumpling is a perfect match. The Ulster pineapple pie is directly from his mother's kitchen, but the addition of rum and pink peppercorns brings it to the modern table with a little sparkle. Since I suggested earlier that his black pepper spätzle would go well with Maja's beef goulash (page 104), I'll recommend that her garlic potato mousse (page 106) could be used in their stead in this menu. Laura Walker's pickled red cabbage (page 45) wouldn't be long for the plate either.

CRAB DUMPLING WITH NƯỚC CHẤM DIPPING SAUCE

Serves 6

For the dumplings:
250g / 9oz crevettes (shrimp) tails, peeled
1–2 tbsp sweet chilli sauce
250g / 9oz crabmeat
2 litres / 3½ pints / 8 cups oil, for frying

For the batter:
200g / 7oz / 1¼ cups self-raising flour
1 egg
1 bottle of sparkling water (how much you use will depend on the day and the flour)

For the sauce:
1 lime, juiced
2 tbsp turbinado sugar (see Chef's Tip on page 12)
120ml / 4fl oz / ½ cup water
2½ tbsp Vietnamese fish sauce
1 garlic clove, finely chopped
1–2 Thai chillies, thinly sliced

Chef's tip:
The humidity of the day will greatly affect the amount of water bakers use when baking breads. Many people don't consider this. The batter should lightly coat your finger. You'll probably use somewhere around 200–300ml / 7–10½fl oz / ¾–1¼ cups. Make sure it's very cold and mix very little. This will keep gluten from forming and making the batter tough.

Preheat the oven to 200°C / 400°F / gas mark 6.

Place crevettes in the bowl of a food processor and pulse to small chunks. Add a little chilli sauce and process until smooth. Place crabmeat in a large bowl and fold the crevette meat into the crab to incorporate fully.

To make the batter, mix flour, egg and just enough sparkling water to make a smooth, thin batter.

To make the sauce, combine the lime juice, sugar and water, stirring to dissolve the sugar. Taste. It should taste pleasantly of limeade. Adjust to balance the sweet and sour. Add remaining ingredients and set aside.

To make the dumplings, preheat the oil in a large pot to 180°C / 350°F.

Form crab into 2-tablespoon-sized balls, arrange on a baking tray lined with non-stick baking paper. Dip four dumplings at a time into batter and fry in the hot oil for 6 minutes, until golden brown. Remove with a slotted spoon to a wire rack set over a rimmed baking tray to drain.

BRAISED PORK BELLY WITH VANILLA FOAM

Serves 6–8

2kg / 4½lb pork belly, rolled and tied

For the brine:
250g / 9oz / 1 cup kosher or large flaked sea salt

1 orange, peel only

1 lemon, peel only

2 tbsp coriander seeds

5 star anise pods

1 tbsp black peppercorns

5 fresh bay leaves

2 sprigs of fresh rosemary

1 bunch of fresh parsley

3 litres / 5¼ pints / 12 cups water

For the braise:
250g / 9oz carrots, peeled and sliced

1 large onion, peeled and sliced

3 litres / 5¼ pints / 12 cups chicken stock

60g / 2oz / 4 tbsp cold unsalted butter, cut into 4 pieces

For the apples:
50g / 1¾oz / ¼ cup sugar

60ml / 2fl oz / ¼ cup water

2 Pink Lady apples

For the vanilla foam:
2 leaves of gelatine

100ml / 3½fl oz / ⅓ cup + 4 tsp skimmed milk

1 x 2.5cm / 1in vanilla bean, sliced lengthwise

¼ tsp sea salt

pinch of ground white pepper

Chef's tip:
Your butcher will most likely weigh the belly with the ribs still attached, but remove them to roll and tie. Make sure you take those ribs with you. You paid for them and they can be used just like any other pork ribs.

DAY 1

In a large stockpot, add salt, orange and lemon peel, coriander seeds, star anise, peppercorns, bay leaves, rosemary, parsley and water. Bring to the boil, remove from heat and cool to room temperature.

Place pork belly in another large pot, pour cooled brine over to cover – weigh down with an inverted plate if necessary to keep belly submerged. Place in refrigerator for 24 hours.

DAY 2

Preheat the oven to 200°C / 400°F / gas mark 6.

Remove pork belly from brine, rinse in cold water. Submerge in cold water for 30 minutes. Drain.

Place carrots and onions in a large casserole dish with pork belly. Add chicken stock and enough water to barely cover. Bring to a hard simmer on top of the stove. Place in oven, uncovered, and immediately reduce oven temperature to 120°C / 250°F / gas mark ½. Cook for 6 hours. Remove from oven and let cool. Remove pork from cooking liquid. Refrigerate pork and stock separately.

Day 3

For the apples, make a syrup of sugar and water by bringing to a boil and letting cool. Peel and core the apples, cut into very small dice, place in cool syrup.

Preheat the oven to 200°C / 400°F / gas mark 6.

Remove fat from cooking liquid and strain. This stock will be part of the sauce for the pork. Remove string and cut the pork belly into slices 1cm / ½in thick. Lay slices on baking tray. Place in oven for 10–15 minutes to crisp.

To make the vanilla foam, soften the gelatine in 500ml / 18fl oz / 2 cups of warm water.

Place milk into a medium-sized non-reactive saucepan. Scrape seeds from vanilla bean into milk, add empty pod and salt. Warm over medium heat, with a kitchen spoon resting in the saucepan, until it just begins to shimmer. Remove milk from heat and discard vanilla bean.

Drain gelatine sheets and squeeze out excess water. Gently stir sheets into milk with white pepper. Froth using a hand-held blender and set aside to rest in a warm place.

Heat 500ml / 18fl oz / 2 cups of cooking liquid in a saucepan over medium heat and reduce by one third. Stir in the cold butter one piece at a time to emulsify. Set aside.

Place heated slices of pork belly on plate and spoon over some sauce. Add a spoonful of vanilla foam and garnish with the apple pieces.

BLACK PEPPER SPÄTZLE

Serves 6

2 eggs
2 tbsp melted lard or duck fat
120ml / 4fl oz / ½ cup water
120ml / 4fl oz / ½ cup milk
225g / 8oz / 2½ cups plain (all-purpose) flour
½ tsp sea salt, plus extra for boiling
¼ tsp baking powder
1 tbsp coarsely ground black pepper
30g / 1oz / 2 tbsp butter, melted
2 tbsp chopped fresh parsley

In a large bowl, whisk together eggs, lard, water and milk very well.

In a separate bowl, sift together flour, salt and baking powder. Stir in black pepper. Using a wooden spoon, blend the dry ingredients into the wet and beat for about 1 minute. Bring 5 litres / 8¾ pints / 5¼ quarts of heavily salted water to a boil.

Using a spätzle-maker set over boiling water, press one third of the dough at a time into water. When the dumplings float to the top, remove using a slotted spoon to a bowl of very cold water. Bring water back to a boil and repeat until all dough is used.

Chef's tip:
If you do not have a spätzle-making press, the dumplings can be formed by squeezing the dough through a piping bag and snipping them with kitchen scissors or, the traditional method, by flicking bits of dough into the water from a wooden cutting board or a dinner plate.

In between, remove cooked dumplings and shake in a colander to remove excess water. Place into a large bowl and coat each batch with 1 tsp of melted butter. Set aside.

To serve, heat a large non-stick sauté pan over medium–high heat. Add the remaining melted butter and let it sizzle and just begin to turn brown. Add spätzle and toss. Brown for about 2 minutes on one side. Toss and continue to heat for another minute or two. Garnish with chopped fresh parsley and serve.

ULSTER PINEAPPLE PIE

Serves 6–8

For the base:
125g / 4½oz digestive or ginger nut biscuits, ground to fine crumbs
90g / 3oz / 6 tbsp butter, melted
4 tbsp caster (superfine) sugar
¼ tsp ground cinnamon (optional)

For the filling:
1 fresh pineapple, peeled and cut into 1cm / ½in chunks (about 2½ cups prepared)
1 tbsp dark brown sugar
pinch of table salt
¼ tsp pink peppercorns, cracked or crushed, but not ground (optional)
1 tbsp dark rum (optional)
500ml / 18fl oz / 2 cups cream, whipped

Preheat the oven to 190°C / 375°F / gas mark 5.

To make the base, mix biscuit crumbs, melted butter, sugar and cinnamon, if using, until well blended. Press into a 23cm / 9in pie dish. Bake in the oven for 5–7 minutes. Cool completely on a wire rack.

To make the filling, toss the pineapple chunks with the brown sugar, salt and pink peppercorns, if using, in a bowl. Place in a colander set over a bowl for 30 minutes to drain.

Pat the chunks dry on a clean tea towel and place in a bowl. Sprinkle with rum, if using.

In a separate large, cold bowl, whip cream to stiff peaks. Fold whipped cream into pineapple until well distributed.

Pour cream and pineapple into prepared biscuit base – it will mound fairly high. Refrigerate for 1 hour before serving.

Chef's tip:
Ginger snap cookies or graham crackers can be used, if you prefer.

RACHAEL BOYLE

The Charthouse

LUCKY LADDERS AND OPENED DOORS

Rachael Boyle enjoys watching her children on the same west Kerry beaches she herself played as a child

CHEF RACHAEL BOYLE grew up in a B&B guesthouse west of Dingle. Hers was an Irish-speaking, traditional farming family where good-quality food, simply but lovingly prepared, was standard fare. Her early kitchen memories include her mother and grandmother patting batches of scones and cutting them out by the dozens, a job she would soon take over before she headed off to school for the morning.

In her early teens she took her first job in the kitchen of Tigh Uí Chatháin, a pub in Ballyferriter, where she saw the same ingredients that nourished her family – enhanced with a bit of herb or a splash of wine and a dash of spice – bring joy and satisfaction to visiting customers from around the world. 'That was me, hooked!' she tells me, and she went to Killarney to catering college despite the advice of many friends who knew how hard the work of cheffing can be.

From pub food 'Back West', Rachael found herself in the kitchens of Ballynahinch Castle in the Connemara Gaeltacht. She was climbing the culinary ladder very quickly. Working in a kitchen brigade chock-a-block with French and German chefs, Rachael was lucky enough to be under one of the premiere female head chefs in Ireland at the time. She was increasingly seeing not only new produce and ingredients, but with each new step on this ladder she was learning new methods of cookery and ways to deepen and enhance natural flavours without overwhelming them.

From pub grub to fine dining in short order, Rachael headed to Edinburgh to put her own feet to the fire as an agency chef. Agency work is demanding but rewarding for the few young chefs who can handle the pace. You might find yourself in a tech firm's canteen for a few days, then filling in at a busy fine-dining restaurant the next, then jumping in to help cater an event for thousands on another. Each kitchen has its own rules, its own style and its own difficulties. After a year and a half of working under a myriad of chefs in various venues, it was time to head home to Ireland.

Galway was a single-season first stop, but her heart (and her family) was always tugging her to return to the Dingle Peninsula. An opening at a busy pub in Dingle town allowed her to run her first kitchen for a season, and from there she took on the sous chef role at the Dingle Skellig Hotel, where, at the ripe old age of 24, another door of opportunity was opened and she was made head chef.

Quite a few chefs featured in this book were hired by and worked under Rachael during her time as head chef until 2004. One chef in particular sticks out in her memory from those days at 'the Skellig' – a tall, Killybegs-trained Belfast lad who came down for a season and stayed for a few years. Though she rebuffed his romantic advances for a while, when Rachael was ready to move on to a larger hotel

job in Wexford, Michael came along with her and the couple were soon married. After opening a brand-new hotel from the ground up and getting the multi-kitchen premises with nearly 30 staff in Carlow town up and running, she returned to the house she had built in her early twenties to raise her family.

It can be said that there are two kinds of chef in the hotel game: openers and maintainers. Rachael Boyle is definitely an opener. A few months after the birth of her first child, she took on the task of opening the kitchen in Dingle's new hospital. The same skills that one uses to open a hotel – menu development, nutritional analysis, HACCP guidelines, costings and the like – were perfectly suited to the new healthcare kitchen, plus the hours were perfect for a new mother who just couldn't leave the business she loves.

After three years – her longest stint in any one kitchen – she was once again itching for her next challenge. Helping out in her old haunt, the Skellig, she sharpened any skills she felt had dulled, and when the position of head chef at the Charthouse opened in late 2015, she pounced at the chance to get back in the game.

Dingle is a place where the people and the place are woven together to create a fabric far stronger than either is on its own. Chef Rachael Boyle is cut from that fabric. It's who she is and it's that cloth in which she now wraps her family of three children as she introduces them to the same fields where she hunted mushrooms, the same mountains she climbed and the same beaches where she swam in her youth. And who knows – with two talented chefs as parents, those children might be the next culinary generation of the peninsula!

One thing you notice when moving from a large metropolis to a small town like Dingle is that you eat ethnic takeaway a lot less often simply because there isn't a lot of it around. Rachael's menu offers the exotic flavours of a big city in the comfort of your own kitchen. If you want to make the evening 100 per cent vegetarian, skip the prawns in the skewers altogether and double the amount of tofu. With flavours like this, your guests won't miss the meat. If black rice is hard to find, Martin Bealin's perfect basmati rice (page 86) will stand in nearly as well.

IN LIEU OF A TAKEAWAY

starter
Coconut lime prawn and tofu
skewers with kachumber salad

main
Sweet potato curry

sides
Raita
Forbidden black rice
Naan

dessert
Chocolate tart with crème fraîche
ice cream

cocktail suggestion
Passion Fruit Caipiroska (page 260)

beverage suggestion
Witbier such as Hoegaarden or your
favourite Hefeweizen

COCONUT LIME PRAWN AND TOFU SKEWERS WITH KACHUMBER SALAD

Serves 6

For the kachumber salad:

1 small red onion, finely diced

3 medium plum tomatoes, quartered, seeded and finely diced

1 cucumber, peeled, seeded and finely diced

5 red radishes, washed well and finely diced

1 hot green chilli, ribbed, seeded and finely chopped (bird's-eye chilli if you can find it, but a Serrano chilli would work fine)

½ bunch coriander (cilantro), finely chopped

¼ tsp fine sea salt

¼ tsp freshly ground black pepper

¼ tsp cayenne pepper (optional)

1–2 tsp lime juice, to taste

For the skewers:

350ml / 12fl oz / 1⅓ cups coconut milk

3 limes, zested and juiced

3 garlic cloves, finely chopped or crushed

2 fresh chillies, finely chopped (keep the ribs and seeds in if you like it hot, discard if not)

6 tbsp fish sauce

6 tbsp soy sauce or tamari

18 large Dingle Bay prawn tails, peeled and deveined

3 x 300g / 10½oz packages of firm tofu, drained and cut into 18 'fingers'

12 metal or bamboo skewers

40g / 1½oz / ⅓ cup toasted sesame seeds

1 bunch of fresh coriander (cilantro), washed, with about 6cm / 2½in of the stems still attached

1 lime, cut into 6 wedges, to serve

To make the salad, toss all ingredients together in a large bowl. Taste for seasoning and heat. Correct with salt, pepper and lime juice. Set aside. (If the salad seems too hot, a pinch of sugar will tame it a bit, but don't use too much or salad will become too sweet.)

To make the skewers, whisk coconut milk, lime zest and juice, garlic, chilli, fish sauce and soy sauce together in a large bowl. Add prawns and tofu, gently toss to coat well, cover with cling film and refrigerate for 1–2 hours.

If using bamboo skewers, soak in cold water for 30 minutes. Thread three prawns per skewer on six skewers and three pieces of tofu per skewer on six skewers.

In a small saucepan over medium–high heat, bring remaining marinade just to a boil, remove from heat and reserve.

On a preheated barbecue grill or on a hot griddle pan, cook skewers for 2–3 minutes on each side, until hot with nice grill marks. Remove to a warm plate and brush well with reserved marinade.

To serve, mound some salad on plates, arrange one shrimp skewer and one tofu skewer per plate. Top with toasted sesame seeds and garnish with coriander sprigs and lime wedge.

⊚ ⊙ ⊚ ⊙ ⊚ ⊙ ⊚ ⊙ ⊚ ⊙ ⊚ ⊙ ⊚

SWEET POTATO CURRY

Serves 6

For the red curry paste:
2 tsp hot or sweet paprika, depending on your taste
½ tsp ground coriander
½ tsp ground cumin
¼ tsp ground turmeric
pinch of ground cinnamon
pinch of ground cardamom
pinch of sea salt
7 large red chillies, ribbed and seeded (unless you like it fiery hot)
2cm / ¾in piece of fresh ginger, peeled and chopped
2 lemongrass stalks, outer leaves discarded, thinly sliced
3 garlic cloves, chopped
6 shallots, chopped
5 sprigs of fresh coriander (cilantro), stems included
2 tsp anchovy paste

For the curry:

600ml / 1 pint / 2⅓ cups coconut milk

2 heads of pak choi, washed and cut into 5cm / 2in pieces

100g / 3½oz mangetout (snow peas), julienned

2 green bell peppers, julienned

8 large sweet potatoes, peeled and cut into 5cm / 2in dice

4 tbsp rapeseed oil

6 tbsp red curry paste

2 tbsp fish sauce

¼ tsp sea salt

1 tsp brown sugar

4 fresh kaffir lime leaves

1 courgette (zucchini), julienned

500g / 1lb 2oz baby spinach

1 bunch of fresh Thai basil leaves

To make the red curry paste, toast the spices in a small sauté pan over medium–high heat until they become fragrant, about 1 minute. Remove to a cold plate to stop cooking and allow to cool.

Put all ingredients and toasted spices into blender jug and blend thoroughly to a paste. Place in an impermeable (glass or ceramic) dish, cover and refrigerate for up to one week.

To make the curry, remove the cream from the coconut milk (the thickest part at the top of the tin) and set aside.

In a large pot of boiling salted water, blanch pak choi, mangetout and peppers one at a time for about 20 seconds (peppers maybe closer to 1 minute). Shock in ice water and spin or pat dry. Set aside.

In a medium saucepan over medium–high heat, place sweet potatoes and coconut milk. Bring to a boil and reduce heat to medium. Simmer, stirring frequently, until tender, 10–15 minutes. Remove from heat and set aside.

In a heavy wok or casserole (Dutch oven) over high heat, add oil and curry paste. Fry until paste is lightly browned and very fragrant. Add coconut cream and stir to blend. Reduce heat to medium–low. Stir in fish sauce, salt, brown sugar and lime leaves. Add sweet potatoes with coconut milk, blanched vegetables, courgette and spinach. Increase heat to medium–high and bring to boil. Turn off heat and cover for 2 minutes.

Garnish with basil leaves and serve family style with black rice, raita and naan bread.

RAITA

Serves 6

2 cucumbers, peeled, halved lengthwise, seeded and thinly sliced
1 tsp fine sea salt
½ tsp ground black pepper
500g / 1lb 2oz / 2 cups plain Greek-style yogurt
6 tbsp extra virgin olive oil
60ml / 2fl oz / ¼ cup lemon juice
1 garlic clove, finely chopped
2 tbsp finely chopped fresh basil (Thai basil is preferable, but sweet basil will do fine)
2 tbsp finely chopped fresh mint

In a medium bowl, toss cucumber slices with salt and pepper to combine. Transfer to a colander and place over the bowl. Let stand for 30 minutes to drain excess water.

In a large bowl, whisk yogurt, oil, lemon juice, garlic, basil and mint.

Gently squeeze the cucumber over the sink and fold into the yogurt mixture. Correct seasoning with salt and pepper. Cover and refrigerate for up to 24 hours. Serve as condiment with the sweet potato curry.

FORBIDDEN BLACK RICE

Serves 6

575g / 20oz / 3 cups black rice, rinsed well
1½ tsp sea salt
1.3 litres / 2¼ pints / 5¼ cups cold water

In a heavy pot over high heat, combine rice, salt and water and bring to a boil. Reduce heat to low (see the note below) and simmer until grains are tender, about 30 minutes.

Remove from heat, drain any excess water, cover with a clean tea towel and replace the lid. Let stand for 10 minutes.

Note: If using an electric hob (stovetop), have a second burner set to low heat to move the rice to after it has reached a boil. Electric heating elements take too long to cool down when cooking rice.

NAAN

Makes 8

2 egg yolks
170g / 6oz / ⅔ cup Greek-style plain yogurt
250ml / 9fl oz / 1 cup ice-cold water
6 tbsp + 2 tsp Irish rapeseed oil, plus extra for greasing
560g / 19¾oz / 3¾ cups plain (all-purpose) flour
2½ tsp caster (superfine) sugar
1 tsp instant or rapid-rise yeast
2½ tsp table salt
clean spray bottle with water
45g / 1½oz / 3 tbsp unsalted butter, softened
1 small handful (about ¼ cup) coriander (cilantro), finely chopped (optional)

In a medium-sized bowl, whisk together egg yolks, yogurt, water and 6 tbsp oil. Set aside.

In the bowl of a food processer, add flour, sugar and yeast and pulse three or four times to combine. With processor running, slowly pour in the yogurt mixture and process until no dry flour remains, about 10–15 seconds. Turn off and let stand for 12 minutes.

Remove processor lid, sprinkle surface of dough with salt, cover and process for 30–60 seconds, until the dough pulls from the sides of the bowl and a sticky dough ball begins to form.

Transfer dough to lightly floured work surface and knead for about 1 minute, until smooth.

Shape into a tight ball and place in a large oiled bowl. Cover with a clean, warm, damp tea towel and set aside to rise, at room temperature, for 30–45 minutes.

Uncover the bowl, lift the edge of the dough closest to you from the side of the bowl and fold to the centre. Turn the bowl 90° and repeat eight times. Cover the bowl tightly with cling film and allow to rise for a further 30 minutes. Repeat the folding process, cover and let rise a third time for 30 minutes.

Preheat the oven to 90°C / 200°F / gas mark ¼. Place an ovenproof platter in the middle of the oven to warm up. Lightly oil a baking tray.

Transfer dough to lightly floured work surface, punch down and divide into eight equal pieces. Form each piece of dough into a smooth, tight ball. Place dough balls on the oiled baking tray, at least 5cm / 2in apart, oil a piece of cling film and cover the dough balls loosely – oiled side down – and let stand 15–20 minutes to rest.

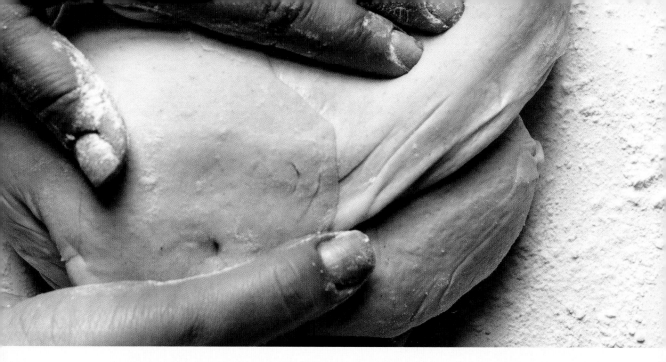

Heat a large cast-iron frying pan, ideally one that's about 30.5cm / 12in in diameter, over medium heat.

Lightly flour a work surface and, one ball at a time, flatten the dough into a 23cm / 9in round, using more flour as needed to prevent sticking. A rolling pin can be used as well, if you like.

Shake off excess flour and prick the surface of the dough about two dozen times with a dinner fork.

Add 1 teaspoon of oil to the preheated pan and swirl around to coat. Once oil is shimmering, wipe the oil completely out of the frying pan with a piece of kitchen paper (paper towel).

Mist the top of the formed dough with a spritz of water and place in the pan, moistened side down, mist the dough again and cover. 'Bake' on the hob for 2–4 minutes, until large brown spots appear on the bottom surface of the naan. Flip and cover. Continue to bake for 2–3 more minutes (if the naan puffs, prick with fork to deflate). While one naan is baking, shape the next.

Flip the naan onto the preheated plate so that the side that was last facing the heat is now on top. Rub with 1 teaspoon of softened butter and sprinkle with finely chopped coriander, if using. Cover loosely with foil and put in the oven.

Repeat the process until all eight naans are baked. Serve immediately.

CHOCOLATE TART WITH CRÈME FRAÎCHE ICE CREAM

Serves 6–8

For the ice cream:
175g / 6¼oz / ¾ cup + 1 tbsp caster (superfine) sugar
80ml / 3fl oz / ⅓ cup water
500g / 1lb 2oz / 2 cups crème fraîche

For the pastry:
275g / 9¾oz / 1¾ cups plain (all-purpose) flour
100g / 3½oz / ¾ cup icing (powdered) sugar
100g / 3½oz / ½ cup cold butter
2 eggs

For the filling:
400g / 14oz dark chocolate drops (70–80% cocoa solids)
250ml / 9fl oz / 1 cup double (heavy) cream
100g / 3½oz / ½ cup caster (superfine) sugar

To decorate:
sprigs of fresh mint

To make the ice cream, whisk sugar and water together in a small saucepan over a high heat until dissolved. Remove from heat and cool completely.

In a large bowl whisk crème fraîche and cooled syrup until smooth.

Pour into an ice cream machine and churn until frozen. Transfer to a container and place in freezer for up to two weeks. Remove from freezer 15 minutes before use.

To make the pastry, sift flour and icing sugar together in a large bowl. Add butter and work with fork or fingers until the mixture resembles breadcrumbs. Make a well in the centre, add eggs and mix until a sticky dough forms.

Turn out onto a lightly floured work surface and gently knead two or three times to bring the dough together. Wrap in cling film and refrigerate for at least 30 minutes and up to 24 hours. Take the dough out of the refrigerator about 10 minutes before rolling.

Preheat the oven to 180°C / 350°F / gas mark 4.

Roll dough out to approximately 3mm / ⅛in thickness, transfer and press into a 23cm / 9in tart tin with a removable bottom. 'Dock' the dough by pricking with a fork 40–50 times.

Blind bake the pastry in preheated oven for 20–30 minutes, until golden brown and flaky. Cool completely.

To make the filling, put the chocolate into a large heatproof bowl.

In a small saucepan over medium heat add cream and all but 1 tablespoon of the sugar. Bring to a hard simmer, stirring to dissolve sugar in the cream. Pour hot cream mixture into the chocolate and stir until melted and smooth. Pour into cooled pastry base and sprinkle reserved tablespoon of sugar over the top.

Glaze with a blowtorch.

Leave for 2 hours to set. Remove from tart pan. Serve with crème fraîche ice cream and garnish with mint, if desired.

FERNANDO LOVISETTO

Novecento

OUR ITALIAN NEIGHBOUR

A chef's best friend: Fernando enjoys a brisk walk on Ventry strand with his red setter

LOOKING AT A MAP OF VICENZA, ITALY, you can understand why the tastes of Fernando Lovisetto, owner of Novecento, are broad and rich. His home town is nestled at the base of the Dolomite foothills, midway on the road between Venice and Lake Garda, perfectly situated for fresh and saltwater fish and shellfish, game and abundant produce of almost every kind. Fernando grew up in a chef's dreamland.

Over 100 years ago, Fernando's great-grandfather was the chef at a prestigious technical college with students from all over Italy and Europe. He passed on his love and knowledge of the foods of the world to his daughter, Fernando's *nonna* (grandmother), who was like a second mother to Fernando because his parents worked long shifts in a local factory. Though she cooked mostly regional cuisine, she did so with the hand of someone who had grown up with broader tastes.

In the post-war Italy of Fernando's youth, meat was a once-a-month luxury, but polenta made from Maranello corn, escargots gathered and fed on cucumbers and

nettles, risotto with mushrooms foraged from the forest and eels caught in the river would have been typical family fare. These homely dishes now garner top price at white-tablecloth eateries around the world, but Fernando tells me that they're not as good as when he had them cooked on a wood-burning stove.

Fernando met his wife, a Cork woman, in 1987 while she was working abroad as a teacher in his home town. He was a foreman in a factory for 27 years, but his true love was cooking Saturday dinner for friends, Sunday lunch for extended family or even a meal for himself after a long workday.

Fernando's wife, Orla, moved to the Dingle Peninsula first in 1998 and opened a small café in Ballyferriter to test the waters, as Ireland in the 1990s was a friendlier country than Italy in which to open a new restaurant. Fernando followed in 1999 with a vanload of Italian ingredients and some advice from a chef friend in Venice, and opened Novecento Italian Restaurant that spring.

The ingredients were the most difficult part of opening an Italian restaurant in the wilds of west Kerry. Cheeses are different, the names of cuts and the way that meat is cut is different, even ingredients that were imported from Italy at the time were inferior to what he could find if he took his van on the ferry and drove to his home country himself.

He continued making quarterly runs to Italy for the best-quality ingredients until he opened a small pizzeria in 2003. At that point he developed relationships with suppliers and began having pallets of goods shipped to Ireland, as he couldn't get away from his busy businesses. In 2008 he shuttered the restaurant and concentrated on pizza alone, though his two Cork city locations still serve fresh pasta and salads as well.

His love of handmade food comes through even in a simple slice of cheese pizza. He learns something new about ingredients or tastes or techniques every day, he tells me. It's a great joy to give friends foods that they have never eaten before. An even greater joy for Fernando is trying out an ingredient, a dish or a cooking method he has never used before. He is always learning and always experimenting, but remains true to his roots in the north-east of Italy.

Fernando started in the food business as his second career because he likes to eat good food. He enjoys searching for the highest-quality ingredients, he loves to create wonderful dishes with his hands like the long, slow-cooked food his *nonna* made for him when he was a boy and he relishes the chance to sit down with friends over a meal of great food and good wine and talk about food into the early hours of the morning.

Liver isn't what many people would consider dinner-party food. If your mother cooked liver like I remember it from my childhood, you might not even consider it food fit for people at all. This dish, however, is something special. If you can't find liver of wild boar (and it's worth searching out), pork liver will do. If you can't find that, then fresh lamb's liver is nearly as good. Calf's liver or beef liver would be too strong for this rustic but delicate dish. Olivier Beaujouan's lamb's lettuce and beetroot salad with chive vinaigrette (page 110) would be a good accompaniment to this rich menu if you'd like something light.

FROM THE ITALIAN COUNTRYSIDE

starter
Potato gnocchi with sage butter

main
Braised liver of wild boar

sides
Polenta

dessert
Bussolà vicentino (Marsala cake from Fernando's home town)

cocktail suggestion
Grapefruit Negroni (page 257)

wine suggestion
Valpolicella Ripasso

POTATO GNOCCHI WITH SAGE BUTTER

Serves 6

1kg / 2¼lb floury potatoes, peeled and halved
330g / 11½oz / 2¼ cups plain (all-purpose) flour, plus extra for dusting
1 egg
pinch of salt
45g / 1½oz / 3 tbsp butter
1 shot of grappa (Italian brandy) or Dingle vodka

For the sage butter:
100g / 3½oz / ½ cup salted butter
10 fresh sage leaves
100g / 3½oz / 1 cup grated Parmigiano-Reggiano cheese
freshly ground black pepper

Place potatoes in a steamer basket set over 10cm / 4in of boiling salted water. Steam until fork tender, rinsing after about 5 minutes to remove excess starch. Remove steamer basket and cover with a clean tea towel for 2 minutes to absorb steam.

Mash potatoes through a food mill or ricer (can be done with a hand masher, but make sure there are absolutely no lumps). Add flour, egg, salt and butter. Stir to blend. Add grappa and mix until smooth and thick.

Divide dough in four. Lightly dust a work surface with flour. Roll each piece of dough into a rope about the thickness of your thumb. Using a sharp knife, cut each rope into lengths about twice as long as they are thick. Lay gnocchi evenly on a baking tray.

In a large pot over high heat, bring 5 litres / 8¾ pints / 5¼ quarts of heavily salted water to a boil. Add one quarter of the gnocchi to the water and boil until they float. Remove from water using a slotted spoon and place on a large plate. Repeat for all the gnocchi.

In a large sauté pan over medium–high heat, melt butter until it begins to stop sizzling. Add sage leaves and cook until the colour deepens and they become very fragrant.

Add gnocchi and toss in hot sage butter. Divide between six warm plates and top with grated cheese and black pepper.

BRAISED LIVER OF WILD BOAR

Serves 6

60ml / 2fl oz / ¼ cup olive oil

30g / 1oz / 2 tbsp butter

800g / 1¾lb yellow onions, chopped into 5mm / ¼in dice

1 litre / 1¾ pints / 4 cups beef stock

100g / 3½oz / ⅔ cup plain (all-purpose) flour

salt and freshly ground black pepper

800g / 1¾lb liver of wild boar (or pork or lamb's liver), cut into slices 1cm / ½in thick

1 bunch of fresh parsley, leaves only, chopped

In a large ovenproof casserole (Dutch oven) over medium heat, add olive oil and butter. Heat until butter stops foaming. Add chopped onion and a pinch of salt. Cook, stirring occasionally, until onions soften and begin to turn gold in colour, not brown.

Add beef stock and bring to a simmer. Reduce heat to low and cook, uncovered, for 40 minutes.

Place flour, salt and pepper on a large plate and mix. Roll slices of liver in flour and shake off excess. Place slices into simmering stock and cook for 5 minutes – do not overcook. Taste and correct for seasoning. Serve over warm polenta and garnish with parsley.

POLENTA

Serves 6

1.5 litres / 2½ pints / 6 cups cold water

1 tbsp sea salt

500g / 1lb 2oz stone-ground polenta flour

3 tbsp olive oil

15g / ½oz / 1 tbsp butter (optional)

While stirring water in a heavy-bottomed pot over a medium-high heat, add salt and then slowly pour in the polenta flour in order to avoid lumps. Stir in olive oil, reduce to medium heat and cook for 45 minutes, stirring often so polenta does not stick or clump. Stir in butter, if using.

BUSSOLÀ VICENTINO
(MARSALA CAKE FROM FERNANDO'S HOMETOWN)

Serves 6–8

250g / 9oz / 1⅔ cups plain (all-purpose) flour
50g / 1¾oz / 3tbsp granulated sugar
pinch of table salt
20g / ¾oz fresh yeast
75g / 2½oz / 5 tbsp butter
3 eggs
2 tbsp dry Marsala wine
2 tbsp coarse decorating sugar

Sift flour into a large mixing bowl. Stir in sugar and salt.

In a small bowl, mash yeast with 2 tablespoons of warm water. Make a well in the centre of the flour and add 45g / 1½oz / 3 tbsp of the butter, melted. Stir to combine. Add yeast, two eggs and one yolk (reserve the white for brushing the batter) and beat with a wooden spoon.

Add a few drops of the Marsala at a time as you beat the batter for about 5 minutes (yes, your arm is going to be tired!).

Use the remaining 30g / 1oz / 2 tablespoons of the butter to grease a ring-shaped baking mould (an angel food cake mould works well). Spread the batter around the mould. Brush with egg white and top with decorating sugar. Place a clean tea towel over the batter and let it rise in a warm place for 90 minutes.

Preheat the oven to 190°C / 375°F / gas mark 5.

Bake for 30 minutes. Cool in the mould on a wire rack for 20 minutes, then remove from the baking mould and allow to cool completely.

Serve with strong coffee or even better, sweet Marsala or Vin Santo wine.

Chef's tip:
If fresh yeast is difficult to come by it can be substituted with 1 tsp of dry – not instant or quick-rise – yeast.

NIALL Ó CONCHÚIR

An Canteen

FOOD WITH A VIEW OF HOME

*'Back West' on his family's farm
with a view is where Niall
learnt, and still loves, to cook*

THE Ó CONCHÚIR KITCHEN was seldom not abuzz with cooking activities when Niall was growing up, whether it was for Irish-language students, farmhands, B&B guests or film crews. Mrs Ó Conchúir denies to this day that she does much cooking, though Niall hardly remembers a time in his youth without twenty or thirty extra mouths gathered for her traditional Irish cooking in their home in the townland of An Ghráig at the far west end of our peninsula.

Idle hands led to idle minds in the house as well as the townland, so Niall and his four siblings were kept busy. They were brought up to finish their chores quickly and then head off to see which farmer or fisherman or builder might need an extra set of hands on any particular day. From early on, however, Niall had a taste – a *blas* as they say in the west Kerry Gaeltacht – for working in the kitchen.

It may have been this *blas* that he took with him when he moved to Barcelona when he was 17. Though he worked the counter in a variety of Irish bars, it was the food of the city that made him want to stay. Taking cookery classes and visiting the kitchens of the mothers and grandmothers of new friends, Niall learned about ingredients, flavours and amalgamations of cooking styles the likes of which he'd never dreamed of back home in Dingle.

It was often in the matriarchal kitchens of local chefs' families where Niall would learn the most. When I asked him how he got to know chefs' mothers and grandmothers, he simply said, 'I was working in bars. Chefs drink. That's how I met chefs and got invited to *abuela*'s house on Sunday afternoons.'

This early culinary scrapbooking continued to expand his mind when Niall began dating a Frenchwoman and started to split his time between Spain and France, with trips around the Gulf of Lion region, from Spain, through France and into Italy.

The jump from avid hobby cook and culinary basking shark raking in as much kitchen knowledge as he could garner to opening a successful restaurant is a pretty major leap. For Niall, however, it was more something he stumbled into.

At the same time as the lease he held on a licensed public house was ending, his parents were set to celebrate their sixtieth wedding anniversary. It seemed fitting to use his last night as a publican to throw a party for staff and regulars as well as host his parents' party at the same time.

At 10:30 p.m. on the night before the party, Niall received a life-changing phone call from the chef he'd hired to cater the event, saying that he wouldn't be able to do it. Early the next morning, with less than twelve hours to go till the party started, Niall filled two trolleys at the local grocery, then prepared and cooked a menu of four starter courses, five mains and seven desserts for over 100 people. It was a scale of cookery he'd never attempted before and the rush of it all caught him and never let him go.

With the intention of opening a small café, Niall and his younger brother, Brian, took over the rent on a small space on Dykegate Lane. Brian put a coat of paint on the place while Niall headed up to Dublin for a two-week *stage* in a well-known kitchen with a chef friend who helped him lay the culinary course for their restaurant, An Canteen.

Taking influences from the international Slow Food movement as well as from Niall's travels in Asia, An Canteen's food adapted home recipes he grew up enjoying 'Back West' with ingredients and influences from around the globe. It was an instant hit, and even though it was off the beaten track and hard to find, it soon became the go-to place for families and foodies.

Niall was the only chef I spoke to who noted that in addition to the ingredients of the peninsula, the weather in Dingle also plays a part in the food he cooks. When people think of comfort foods, the idea of barbecue or *à la minute* cookery doesn't come to mind; but slowly cooked, big-flavoured, homey dishes like Niall's braised beef cheeks or confit of pork belly somehow fit like a knitted jumper by the fire on a damp evening.

WEST KERRY SUNDAY LUNCH

starter
Pan-fried mackerel with
pickled vegetables

main
Braised lamb shoulder

sides
Potato gratin
Roasted root vegetables

dessert
Lime cheesecake

cocktail suggestion
Seaside Royale (page 262)

wine suggestion
Ribera del Duero

As you might be able to tell from Niall's story, he loves side dishes. The accompaniments at one of his parties might outshine the main on the groaning sideboard. The lovely mackerel starter that Niall offers could set the stage for a buffet that includes Caroline Danaher's curly kale colcannon (page 194), my sweet potato and three-mustard dish (page 56) and Laura Walker's pickled red cabbage (page 45). Better advise your guests to wear their stretchy trousers!

PAN-FRIED MACKEREL WITH PICKLED VEGETABLES

Serves 6

50g / 1¾oz / ⅓ cup plain (all-purpose) flour

1 tbsp sea salt

1 tsp black pepper

6 small fresh mackerel fillets

2 tbsp vegetable oil, for frying

salt and freshly ground black pepper

For the pickled vegetables:

1 cucumber, thinly sliced

1 red onion, thinly sliced

1 small beetroot, peeled and sliced very thinly (use a mandolin if you have one)

2 tbsp capers, rinsed

1 punnet (basket) of cherry tomatoes, halved

For the brine:

60ml / 2fl oz / ¼ cup red wine vinegar

50g / 1¾oz / ¼ cup granulated sugar

1 tsp sea salt

1 tsp black peppercorns

For the salad:

60ml / 2fl oz / ¼ cup olive oil

1 tbsp finely chopped fresh coriander (cilantro) leaves

120g / 4¼oz mixed baby salad leaves

Place cucumber and red onion in a bowl and lightly salt. Toss and place in colander over a bowl. Place beetroot, capers and tomato halves in a large non-reactive bowl. Leave while making brine for veg.

Mix vinegar, sugar, salt and peppercorns together until salt and sugar are dissolved. Pour over beetroot and stir to combine. Add cucumber and onions. Set aside for 2 hours. Drain and reserve 2 tablespoons of the brine.

Make a vinaigrette by placing the reserved 2 tablespoons of the brine in a small bowl and whisking in the olive oil in a slow, steady stream. Stir in the chopped coriander and set aside.

Mix flour, salt and pepper on a plate.

Heat a large non-stick frying pan over medium–high heat and add 1 tablespoon of oil. Working in batches, coat three fillets of mackerel in seasoned flour. Shake off excess.

Place the fish in the hot pan, skin side up. Cook for 1½–2 minutes per side. Remove and keep warm while you repeat with the other three fillets.

Toss salad leaves with a few tablespoons of dressing to taste. Arrange leaves on plates along with pickled vegetables. Top with mackerel fillets.

Chef's tip:
The brine Niall uses for pickling can be used for quick pickles of several vegetables. Green beans, okra, sugarsnap peas, samphire and many more veggies benefit from a quick pickle in this fashion. Play with the whole spices as well. Allspice, clove, cumin, coriander ... the list is nearly endless.

BRAISED LAMB SHOULDER

Serves 6–8

1 lamb shoulder, boned, rolled and tied (ask your butcher to do this)

2 tbsp Irish rapeseed oil

2 onions, cut into 2.5cm / 1in dice

1 head of garlic, cut in half across the equator

1 x 400g / 14oz can of chopped tomatoes

1 litre / 1¾ pints / 4 cups chicken stock

½ bottle of dry red wine

1 sprig of fresh rosemary

salt and freshly ground black pepper

DAY 1

Preheat the oven to 120°C / 250°F / gas mark ½.

Season shoulder very well with salt and pepper. In a heavy-bottomed casserole (Dutch oven), heat oil over medium–high heat until just smoking. Sear lamb on all sides for at least 4 minutes per side, without moving it to get a nice brown crust. Remove lamb and lower heat to medium.

Add onion and garlic. Stir for about 1 minute. Deglaze with wine and scrape up the browned bits. Add remaining ingredients and bring to a simmer.

Return lamb to the pot and add some cold water if needed to just cover the lamb. Bring to a simmer. Cover and place in the oven for 3 hours. Remove from oven and let the lamb cool, uncovered, in the liquid for about 1 hour.

Lay several layers of cling film about 1 metre long by 60cm wide / 3 ft by 2 ft evenly on a work surface (the kitchen table works well). Remove the lamb to a 60cm / 2 ft end of the cling film. Cut and discard all twine. Season well with salt and pepper.

Starting at the closest edge, lift the cling film and roll the lamb into a tight cylinder. Use the excess film on the sides to tighten the roll as you roll it all the way to the top end. Place in the refrigerator overnight.

Strain the cooking liquid, cool and refrigerate overnight.

DAY 2

Preheat the oven to 180°C / 350°F / gas mark 4.

To serve, slice the lamb into portions 5cm / 2in thick. Remove all cling film.

Ladle 120ml / 4fl oz / ½ cup of the cooking liquid onto a rimmed baking tray. Top with slices of lamb and then top each slice with another 60ml / 2fl oz / ¼ cup of cooking liquid. Reheat in oven for about 20 minutes, glazing with more sauce if needed.

POTATO GRATIN

Serves 6–8

15g / ½oz / 1 tbsp butter, for greasing

1 small onion, thinly sliced

200ml / 7fl oz / ¾ cup + 4 tsp cream

200ml / 7fl oz / ¾ cup + 4 tsp chicken stock

2 garlic cloves, pressed

10 floury potatoes, peeled and thinly sliced

2 tsp sea salt

¾ tsp ground black pepper

pinch of ground nutmeg

100g / 3½oz / 1 cup grated mature Cheddar cheese

Preheat the oven to 200°C / 400°F / gas mark 6. Butter an ovenproof baking dish.

In a large pot over medium heat, mix onion, cream, stock and garlic and bring to a simmer. Add potatoes, salt, pepper and nutmeg. Cook for 5–10 minutes, until potatoes just begin to soften. Pour potato mixture into the buttered dish.

Top with grated cheese and bake for about 30 minutes, until potatoes are tender and cheese is browned.

ROASTED ROOT VEGETABLES

Serves 6

6 carrots, chopped into 4cm / 1½in chunks

4 parsnips, chopped into 5cm / 2in chunks

1 head of garlic, cloves peeled and left whole

3 large shallots, peeled and cut into slices 1cm / ½in thick

2 tbsp Irish rapeseed oil or extra virgin olive oil

2 tsp honey

1 tsp fresh thyme leaves

coarse sea salt and freshly ground black pepper

2 tbsp finely chopped fresh parsley or chives, to garnish

Preheat the oven to 200°C / 400°F / gas mark 6. Place a rimmed baking tray in the oven to heat up.

In a large bowl, combine all ingredients (except parsley and chives) and season well. Pour onto the preheated baking tray, return to the oven and reduce the heat to 180°C / 350°F / gas mark 4.

Roast for about 20 minutes, until tender, stirring two or three times during the roasting process. Garnish with the chopped fresh parsley or chives.

LIME CHEESECAKE

Serves 6–8

For the base:
150g / 5¼oz (half a regular packet) digestive biscuits, crushed into fine crumbs
150g / 5¼oz (half a regular packet) gingernut biscuits, crushed into fine crumbs
75g / 2½oz / 5 tbsp melted butter

For the filling:
3½ sheets of gelatine
500g / 1lb 2oz cream cheese, softened
3 tbsp caster (superfine) sugar
5 limes
500ml / 18fl oz / 2 cups cream

To make the base, mix biscuit crumbs and melted butter in a large bowl. Press in an even layer on the bottom of a 23cm–25cm / 9–10in springform tin. Set aside.

To make the filling, soften gelatine sheets in a cup of warm water for 3 minutes.

In a medium-sized bowl, mix cream cheese and sugar until completely incorporated. Zest three of the limes and fold in the zest, then set aside.

Juice all five limes and pour the juice into a small bowl. Drain and squeeze excess liquid from the gelatine. Mix into lime juice and stir to dissolve (you can warm it a little if needed). Stir juice into cream cheese and mix completely.

In a large bowl, whip cream until it reaches soft peaks. Gently fold whipped cream into lime and cream cheese mixture until fully incorporated.

Pour into prepared springform tin, cover with cling film and refrigerate for a minimum of 2 hours or overnight.

Chef's tip:
1 tsp granulated gelatine (about 1 envelope) equals 3 sheets of gelatine.

ED MULVIHILL

Grey's Lane Bistro

FAMILY FIRST

Out of the frying pan and onto the climbing wall. Ed and his son Louka blow off a bit of steam

T HE MENU Ed Mulvihill offers has celebratory notes of the extended holiday he took when he and his life and business partner, Laurence, took their two teenaged children to Cuba and got married. Family is of utmost importance to Ed and Laurence. They work very carefully to balance a busy working life owning and operating a popular bistro while raising children in modern Ireland.

Ed grew up in a large Listowel family of seven children separated by nearly twenty-one years in total on a small farm where everyone pitched in. Working with their father on one project or another, be it digging turf in the bog, mending fences or tending to animals, was the way they all connected. Though their children, Louka and Cécile, work in the Grey's Lane Bistro from time to time, Ed has taken up rock climbing in order to spend time with the kids. It's about as much physical work as farming, but much more fun.

His first trip to Dingle was as part of a residential pre-certification culinary course for three months during a 1990s winter. He then worked under his brother, who had qualified as a chef seven years before and was running a busy restaurant in their home town, and helped him open his own place in Mayo a few years later. Then it was off to France and Germany, where he continued to learn in bustling eateries in Paris and Cologne.

At his first job in Cologne, the owner introduced him to the chef as her new assistant. 'Do you speak German?' the French-accented woman asked. He did not. For the sake of staying family friendly, I'll spare you her response. That was in October, and by December, when the restaurant shuttered for the holidays, they had had their first kiss.

The couple eventually moved to Mayo, back to his brother's restaurant, to get their feet on Irish ground, as Laurence was pregnant with their first child. They had visited Ireland on holidays from Germany and they both loved Dingle, so one spring day, Ed set off as an advance guard to scope out the job prospects. He was introduced to Martin Bealin at the back of a pub. The pair hit it off straight away and crossed the street to reopen Martin's Global Village for the season. Laurence followed a few weeks later and two weeks after that gave birth to their daughter.

Ed gave up the restaurant business a few years on to spend more time with his growing family (they had a son two years later). The couple had set up a small replica of the farm of Ed's youth west of town. As in his childhood days, they kept hens and ducks, grew most of their own vegetables and lived a quiet, simple life as their children grew. During that time, Ed took a job just down the road from their home in

a kiln shed with master potter Louis Mulcahy. 'I went from cooking food for plates to cooking plates for food,' Ed laughs.

With their children in school and Laurence ready to get back into professional kitchens, the two found a serviceable location at the bottom of Goat Street in which to open their own café. Serving simple yet sophisticated dishes with French influences for breakfast, brunch, lunch and seasonally for dinner, Goat Street Café became a local favourite. The cosy dining room made for easy conversation with the next table. Customers became friends and staff became family.

After one successful season they surprised everyone who worked for them with a trip to Paris. Telling them nothing other than to pack for a long weekend and bring passports, the troupe set out for Dublin on an evening bus where they overnighted and played like restaurant staff are known to do. It wasn't until they were all in the check-in lines that they told everyone where they were headed.

As testament to that family atmosphere, many of the Goat Street staff moved with the couple when they shifted location in 2015 to the purpose-built location where Grey's Lane Bistro now is.

Not every dinner party has to be a *dinner* party. A weekend brunch with houseguests is a perfect way to set the stage for exploring or puttering away the day. One of the fun parts about brunch food is that most people, even novice cooks, can pitch in to make the meal a group effort. Put someone to work on the crêpes while another pair of hands makes the fruit salad, and even the most inexperienced cook can whip together this vinaigrette. A few of Caroline Danaher's salmon sausages (page 190) frying in the pan wouldn't be out of place at Ed's brunch table.

SUNDAY FAMILY BRUNCH

starter
Mojito fruit salad

main
Potato tortilla

side
Honey balsamic marinated vegetables

dessert
Crêpes

cocktail suggestion
Blood Orange and Cava Mimosa or make a 'virgin' option for the kids using sparkling water rather than sparkling wine (page 251)

wine suggestion
More cava!

MOJITO FRUIT SALAD

Serves 6

For the dressing:
3 limes, zested and juiced
2 tbsp turbinado sugar (see Chef's Tip on page 12)
pinch of salt
1 bunch of fresh mint, divided in half, leaves picked
white rum, to taste

For the salad:
½ watermelon, seeded and cut into two-bite-sized chunks
1 cantaloupe, seeded and cut into two-bite-sized chunks
1 pineapple, peeled, cored and cut into bite-sized pieces
1 punnet (basket) of strawberries, washed, hulled and halved
2 kiwi fruit, peeled and cut into 8 wedges
2 bananas, ripe but still firm, peeled and cut into thick coins

Mix all the lime juice, half the zest and all the sugar. Stir until dissolved. Add salt and half the mint leaves and muddle to extract the mint flavour. Strain, taste and add as much rum as you like. Set aside.

Gently toss the fruit together in a large, chilled bowl. Drizzle with the mojito dressing and toss to coat. Toss with half the remaining zest and mint leaves. Decorate with the rest of the mint and zest.

Chef's tip:
Ed's rum-laced fruit salad dressing also goes well drizzled on tropical fruits like papaya and mango.

POTATO TORTILLA

Serves 6

60ml / 2fl oz / ¼ cup Spanish olive oil
4 shallots, peeled and sliced
10 small to medium potatoes, peeled, halved and sliced into very thin half-moons
2 garlic cloves, crushed
1 tsp fresh thyme leaves, finely chopped
6 eggs
2 tbsp cream
salt and freshly ground black pepper

Toppings:
olives, pitted and halved
sun-dried tomatoes, chopped
chorizo slices
goat's cheese pieces

Preheat the grill (broiler) to medium–high.

Heat a large non-stick frying pan on high heat. Add olive oil and shallots, turn heat to low and allow to cook for 10 minutes, making sure they do not colour. Add potatoes, garlic, thyme and season with salt and pepper. Toss to coat with oil and cover. Cook for about 20 minutes, checking and tossing frequently until tender.

Mix the eggs with the cream, add to the potatoes and stir. Still on a low heat and uncovered, use a wooden spoon or heat-resistant spatula to turn in the edges slightly and shake the pan as the eggs are cooking.

When the eggs are set but still soft, scatter over your desired toppings and put under the grill for a minute or two, until slightly browned.

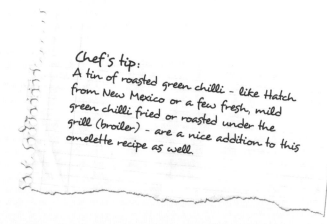

Chef's tip:
A tin of roasted green chilli - like Hatch from New Mexico or a few fresh, mild green chilli fried or roasted under the grill (broiler) - are a nice addition to this omelette recipe as well.

HONEY BALSAMIC MARINATED VEGETABLES

Serves 6–8

120ml / 4fl oz / ½ cup balsamic vinegar
2 tbsp honey
1 red onion, sliced
1 punnet button mushrooms
2 garlic cloves, sliced
1 tbsp good-quality Irish rapeseed oil
2 tbsp soy sauce
1 cucumber, peeled, seeded and cut into slices 2.5cm / 1in thick
1 punnet (basket) of cherry tomatoes, washed and halved
1 red bell pepper, seeded and sliced
salt and freshly ground black pepper

Preheat the oven to 200°C / 400°F / gas mark 6.

In a small non-reactive saucepan, combine vinegar, honey and red onion. Bring to a boil, remove from heat and set aside to cool.

In a bowl, toss mushrooms and garlic with rapeseed oil, season and roast in hot oven for about 10 minutes. Remove and cool slightly.

Slice the mushrooms, place in a small bowl along with the garlic. Toss with soy sauce and reserve.

In a large bowl, combine cucumber and tomatoes with balsamic and honey mixture. Toss to coat.

Add mushrooms and garlic with any soy sauce that hasn't been absorbed. Stir in sliced red bell pepper.

Chef's tip:
Use the roasted, marinated mushroom part of this recipe on its own as a side for grilled steaks and chops.

CRÊPES

Serves 6

225g / 8oz / 1½ cups plain (all-purpose) or gluten-free flour
6 eggs
30g / 1oz / 2½ tbsp caster (superfine) sugar
75g / 2½oz / 5 tbsp melted butter
460ml / 16fl oz / 1¾ cups + 2 tbsp milk
pinch of salt
1 capful of vanilla extract
vegetable oil, for cooking

Serving suggestions:
soft butter
caster sugar
squeeze of lemon juice
fresh fruit
chocolate chips
Nutella
sautéed apples
whipped cream
maple syrup

Blitz all ingredients apart from the oil with a hand-held blender and pass through a sieve.

Heat a large crêpe pan or non-stick frying pan over medium–high heat. Add a few drops of oil and wipe with a piece of kitchen paper (paper towel). Add about half a ladle of batter to the pan. Tilt the pan around to spread the batter. Cook for 1–2 minutes. When the edges start to dry and brown, flip and cook for another minute or two. Experiment with the heat and batter quantities at this stage, as the less batter you use, the better the result.

Stack the crêpes on a warm plate and cover with a clean tea towel to keep them from drying out. Serve warm with your chosen toppings.

Chef's tip:
A capful measure of vanilla extract is usually
½ tsp.

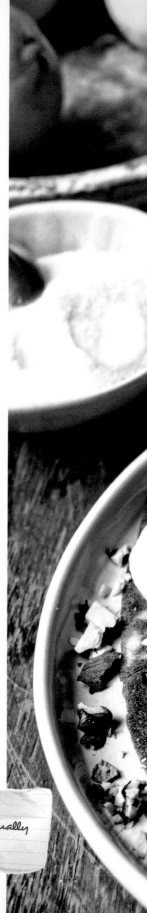

185

CAROLINE DANAHER
The Boatyard

THE PERFECT MATCH

'Dingle Darcy' on a catch-and-cook cruise out of Dingle Harbour

CAROLINE 'DARCY' Danaher's mum, Mary O'Connor, left The Wood, Dingle, for the Lisdoonvarna Matchmaking Festival, met a man and didn't come back. Years later, her daughter, Darcy, did return.

With a grandmother locally renowned for her baked goods and a mother whose Sunday roasts are the stuff of family lore, it's no wonder that Caroline's early memories are full of burnt sugar and black treacle breads, buttered cabbages and roasted chickens. One of her early memories is her 'invention' of the chicken salad sandwich when she was just tall enough to reach the kitchen countertop.

Growing up as the middle of five children, it was Caroline who directed her brothers and sisters in culinary adventures when her parents went out at the weekend. They'd hide ingredients in various presses and cabinets around the house and try something new nearly every week. 'We'd open up all the windows and spray the place with air freshener to hide the fact that we'd been frying doughnuts or baking cakes,' she told me. 'It was practice for my Home Economics course in secondary school.'

After her first job working as a waitress and doing a bit of washing-up in the local hotel in Clare and summers at her uncle's pub back on the Dingle Peninsula, she was so enamoured with the profession that she applied and was accepted to the national chef's certification programme ... until the administrators realised that she was two years too young to enter.

With the mentorship of a successful Limerick restaurant owner, Caroline, who was a new mother by this point, worked her way around the front of the house and eventually into a cook's role, which she relished. When the time came for her daughter to enter school, she decided to move to Dingle and introduce her child to the place she had loved since she was a young one visiting and working during summer holidays. A sous chef position opened at the busy golf club at Ceann Sibéal, so although her co-workers gave her two months, tops, before they expected her to tire of west Kerry, mother and daughter packed up, left Limerick and moved 'Back West'.

Though summers were busy at the golf club, west Kerry winters aren't conducive to very many golf outings, so the kitchen was shuttered. In order to make ends meet during the long off-season, Caroline would walk the 10km round trip every day to Louis Mulcahy's pottery to make tiles and napkin rings. Feeling like Peig Sayers, blown against the hedgerows every day, she loved the work as a way of keeping her hands and her mind busy as she learned new skills.

The unfortunate illness of a business partner led Caroline to go from cook to owner of a small workmen's café that she ran for five years before the lease was up and her daughter was old enough to look after herself. That's when Caroline finally got the opportunity to get her formal culinary education through a total-immersion course at the Tralee IT. Little did she know that the next eight years would find her continuing through an honours degree and on to master's studies.

Not many students enter their studies with as much experience as Caroline did, so it's no surprise that her work placement while at college was as a head chef in first the Marina Inn and then in the Boatyard, where she stayed on after her degree.

Caroline's mother left Dingle to find her perfect match. In career, love and now three children, Caroline has certainly found hers in Dingle, over and over again.

I've often said that guinea fowl is the perfect game for people who find game too strong and for people who find chicken too bland. You'll need to put in a special order for them from your butcher, but it's worth the extra bit of effort. Buy whole guinea fowl and break them down (or have your butcher do it) and the legs and thighs can be used in place of rabbit in Eric Maillard's menu (page 202). Just for fun, you could serve Julian Wyatt's quail Scotch eggs and wilted spinach (page 236) alongside the breasts and ask your guests which came first.

A FANCY FAMILY FEAST

starter
Salmon sausage with creamed leeks

main
Guinea fowl supremes with hunter's sauce

sides
Curly kale colcannon

dessert
Strawberry and vanilla semifreddo

cocktail suggestion
Dingle Dog or Sparkling Pear Punch
(pages 254 and 265)

wine suggestion
Chablis

SALMON SAUSAGE WITH CREAMED LEEKS

Serves 6

For the sausage:
600g / 1lb 5oz salmon fillet, skinned, finely chopped and very well chilled
1 egg yolk
pinch of cayenne pepper
100ml / 3½fl oz / ⅓ cup + 4 tsp double (heavy) cream, well chilled
100g / 3½oz smoked salmon, finely chopped
2 tsp snipped fresh chives
1 tbsp good-quality Irish rapeseed oil
15g / ½oz / 1 tbsp butter

For the creamed leeks:
15g / ½oz / 1 tbsp butter
2 small leeks, washed well and thinly sliced
100ml / 3½fl oz / ⅓ cup + 4 tsp cream
60g / 2oz smoked salmon, diced
1 tsp chiffonaded fresh basil (leaves stacked, rolled tightly and thinly sliced)
salt and freshly ground black pepper
snipped fresh chives

To make the salmon sausage, place the salmon in a food processor and pulse four or five times, scraping down halfway through. It should be like coarse mince. Season to taste, add egg yolk and cayenne pepper, blend until smooth. Scrape down. With the processor running, slowly add the cream. When fully incorporated, turn off machine and fold in smoked salmon and snipped chives to distribute evenly.

Place a double thickness of cling film on the worktop that is about 20cm x 23cm / 8in x 10in in size (you will do this 12 times).

Spoon one twelfth of the salmon mousse (approximately 1 tablespoon) into the centre of the cling film and make a small rectangle, about 2.5cm / 1in in height. Fold the side of the cling film closest to you over the mousse and roll away from you tightly. Twist the ends to tighten and seal. Repeat with the remaining mixture to make 12 sausages in total. Refrigerate for at least 30 minutes and up to 24 hours.

Chef's tip:
Use cold-smoked or gravlax salmon for the sausages as hot-smoked salmon's texture would not fit the dish. Hot-smoked, however, would be nice in the creamed leeks if you happen to have both kinds on hand.

Bring a pan of water to a simmer, poach the salmon sausage (yes, still wrapped in cling film, but the water isn't hot enough to melt it, so worry not), turning as needed, for 6 minutes or until firm to touch. Remove the sausages carefully to prevent them breaking and shock in a large bowl of ice water for about 10 minutes. Place in the refrigerator until needed.

To make the creamed leeks, melt oil and butter together in a large sauté pan over a medium–low heat. Add sliced leeks and a pinch of salt. Cook, stirring often, to soften, 3–4 minutes, do not let them colour. Add cream and increase heat to medium–high, stirring so the cream does not burn, and bring to a boil. Stir in smoked salmon, reduce heat to medium and simmer until reduced to desired consistency. Remove from heat, stir in basil and season to taste.

To serve, remove salmon sausages from their cling film casings.

In a large non-stick sauté pan over medium–high heat, melt oil and butter. When butter stops sizzling, add sausages and cook until warmed through and browned all over. Drain on kitchen paper (paper towel).

Spoon creamed leeks into the centre of warmed plates. On each plate, carefully arrange two salmon sausages as desired and garnish with chives.

GUINEA FOWL SUPREMES WITH HUNTER'S SAUCE

Serves 6

30g / 1oz / 2 tbsp butter, softened

½ lemon, zested and juiced

1 bunch of fresh flat-leaf parsley, leaves washed, picked and roughly chopped

large pinch of paprika

6 split guinea fowl or chicken breasts, bone-in, with wings still attached – your butcher can cut these for you

2 tbsp Irish rapeseed oil

15g / ½oz / 1 tbsp butter

salt and freshly ground black pepper

For the hunter's sauce:

100ml / 3½fl oz / ⅓ cup + 4 tsp unoaked dry white wine

150g / 5¼oz mushrooms, thinly sliced

2 shallots, thinly sliced

15g / ½oz / 1 tbsp butter

500ml / 18fl oz / 2 cups beef stock

3 tomatoes, deseeded and diced

1 tbsp finely chopped fresh tarragon

1 tsp cornflour (cornstarch)

2 tsp water

2 tbsp finely chopped fresh parsley

Chef's tip:
This hunter's sauce is a variation of the classic French sauce chasseur. Normally used with game meats and birds, it's also excellent with beef, pork, chicken and veal dishes.

To prepare the guinea fowl, mix butter, lemon zest, half the lemon juice, parsley, paprika, salt and pepper in a small bowl. Gently lift the skin of each breast away from the meat, spread or pipe 1 teaspoon of the flavoured butter under the skin. Stretch the skin back in place and massage to distribute butter evenly. Cover and chill for 30 minutes or up to a day in advance.

Preheat the oven to 200°C / 400°F / gas mark 6. Remove breasts from refrigerator 10–20 minutes before cooking.

In an ovenproof frying pan over medium–high heat, melt oil and butter together until foaming. Season breasts with salt and pepper. Place breasts in the pan, skin side down, and baste constantly with the butter until starting to brown. Turn the breasts over and place the pan in the preheated oven to roast for 25–30 minutes. Rest under a loose tent of foil for 15 minutes while you make the sauce.

To make the sauce, place the wine in a medium-sized saucepan over a medium heat and reduce by three quarters. Add mushrooms, shallots, butter and beef stock. Bring to a simmer. Add tomatoes and simmer for 5 minutes. Add tarragon.

Mix cornflour and water, add to sauce to thicken slightly. Season with salt and pepper.

To serve, slice the breasts into three or four pieces. Pool sauce on warm plates and top with rested guinea fowl breasts. Garnish with parsley.

CURLY KALE COLCANNON

Serves 6

5–6 large Rooster potatoes, peeled and cut into large chunks
15g / ½oz / 1 tbsp unsalted butter, plus extra for serving
100g / 3½oz curly kale, ribbed and chopped
3 spring onions (scallions), thinly sliced
250ml / 9fl oz / 1 cup milk or cream, warmed
salt and freshly ground black pepper

In a medium pot, cover potatoes by at least 2.5cm / 1in of cold water. Add 2 tablespoons of salt and bring to a boil over medium–high heat. Reduce to medium–low heat and simmer until potatoes are fork tender, 15–20 minutes. Drain in a colander and return to the pot to dry.

While the potatoes are simmering, melt butter in a large pot over medium–high heat. Add kale, stirring to coat with melted butter. Cook for 3–5 minutes, until it has wilted and has given off some of its water. Add the spring onions and cook 1 minute more. Remove from heat.

Mash the potatoes in their pot, adding a little milk or cream, fold in kale and spring onions. Adjust texture with more milk or cream and season with salt, pepper and an extra knob of butter, if desired.

Chef's tip:
Using kale rather than cabbage in this dish deepens the flavour. If you like the look but think the flavour of kale too much for the potatoes, use the dark outer leaves of savoy cabbage in its place. But do try it with kale at least once!

STRAWBERRY AND VANILLA SEMIFREDDO

Serves 6

100ml / 3½fl oz / ⅓ cup + 4 tsp water
100g / 3½oz / ½ cup granulated sugar
125g / 4½oz egg yolks (about 6)
250g / 9oz fresh strawberries, hulled
125g / 4½oz redcurrants, stripped from their stalks
200ml / 7fl oz / ¾ cup + 4 tsp cream
1 vanilla bean, seeds scraped out (reserve the bean for another use)

For the crumble:
30g / 1oz / ⅓ cup cocoa powder
100g / 3½oz / ⅔ cup plain (all-purpose) flour
100g / 3½oz / ½ cup granulated sugar
½ tsp coarse sea salt
100g / 3½oz / ½ cup unsalted butter, cold and cut into cubes

For the coulis:
200g / 7oz / 1 cup caster (superfine) sugar
200ml / 7fl oz / ¾ cup + 4 tsp water
2 large sprigs of fresh mint
250g / 9oz mixed berries (frozen are fine)

To make the semifreddo, add water and sugar to a small saucepan over a high heat. Heat until dissolved. Continue to boil the sugar and water until it reaches 120°C / 250°F.

In the bowl of a stand mixer, whisk egg yolks on full speed until pale, thick and creamy. While the mixer is running, carefully pour the hot sugar solution into the egg yolks – try not to let it touch the side of the bowl or the sugar will not incorporate. Continue whisking on high speed until yolks double in volume and become creamy.

Purée strawberries and redcurrants until smooth, then pass through a fine-mesh sieve to remove the seeds. Fold the purée into the creamy egg and sugar mixture.

Add vanilla seeds to the cream and whip to soft peaks. Fold the vanilla cream into the strawberry mixture. Pour the mixture into a 900g / 2lb loaf tin lined with cling film and freeze overnight.

Preheat the oven to 180°C / 350°F / gas mark 4. Line a baking tray with non-stick baking paper.

To make the crumble, mix cocoa powder, flour, sugar and salt together in a small bowl, rub in the butter until well combined, forming big, dark brown crumbs. Spread mixture onto the lined baking tray, breaking up larger crumbs by flattening them a little. Bake until crisp, about 20 minutes, rotating the tray halfway through baking. Cool completely.

Transfer cooled crumb to a food processor and process into fine, even crumbs. Store in an airtight container for up to one week.

To make the coulis, place sugar and water in a medium saucepan over medium–high heat to dissolve. Remove from heat. Add the mint and leave to infuse for 20 minutes. Strain the mint syrup through a fine-mesh sieve.

Purée mixed berries in blender, stir in 4 tablespoons of the mint syrup and pass through a fine-mesh sieve. Store in an airtight container for up to two days. Stir before using.

To serve, unmould semifreddo loaf from the tin and remove all cling film. Using a long, sharp knife, dipped in warm water between slices, slice semifreddo into 12 equal portions. Place two slices of strawberry semifreddo on a cold plate, decorate with chocolate crumb and drizzle with coulis.

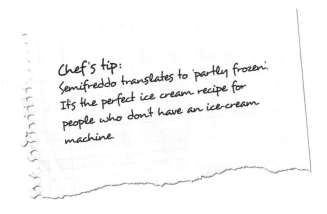

Chef's tip:
Semifreddo translates to 'partly frozen'.
It's the perfect ice cream recipe for
people who don't have an ice-cream
machine.

ERIC MAILLARD
Out of the Blue

CAME FOR THE LANGUAGE, STAYED FOR LOVE

Hands in the soil and head in the kitchen. Eric grows and raises much of his own food for home on his small farm

E RIC MAILLARD grew up in a small region of France not unlike his new home. The north-west department of Mayenne in the Pays de la Loire region where Eric hails from sits at the intersection of Brittany and Normandy near the notch between the English Channel and the Celtic Sea. 'It's green enough, it's rainy enough, it's windy enough and grey in the winter,' he says of the weather. 'It's just like Dingle!'

His father was the engineer for the local water system and his mother was a cook at the local school in their small home town of Martigné-sur-Mayenne. At sixteen, Eric set off for chef's training in Laval, Mayenne's capital, and began the journey that would eventually land him a job as head chef of one of Dingle's favourite restaurants, with a few stops along the way.

One of the stops that brings out the chef's wry smile was his station aboard a French navy ship during his compulsory service. He says that the food was so good on the ship – mind you, Eric was one of the cooks – that he put on nearly two stone in a single two-month patrol.

Before and after his time in the navy, Eric worked in Germany and Austria at mostly French-style restaurants. Learning kitchen German as he worked his way around, he decided to give Dublin a go as a way to learn English while working in the Irish capital.

After six months spending more time having fun and playing than actually learning much English – he worked in a French-speaking kitchen at the time – the 26-year-old decided to head back to Germany and Austria and buckle down to advance his career as a top-class chef (as well as recoup some of the money he had spent in Temple Bar).

Knowing that he would need to learn English if he wanted to realise his potential in the culinary world, Eric took advantage of a tip given to him by some Irish customers in 2001 and sent his CV to someone who told him about a job in the Dingle Skellig Hotel. Little did he know that he was heading to the heart of the west Kerry Gaeltacht – a primarily Irish-speaking region – in order to learn English!

The size, as well as the weather, of Dingle was comparable to his home town, so Eric found it familiar. While the work putting out mostly bar food wasn't very challenging for a chef experienced in fine dining, the experience of the people and the town for one season made an impression. After a break in France and with a job secured for the next summer season in Connemara, Eric stopped in Dingle for a week to catch up with the friends he'd made the year before and to celebrate his thirtieth birthday.

While here he was offered a position at Benner's Hotel, which was remodelling its kitchens at the time. With a month to go before they were ready to open, Eric went to Connemara to help find a replacement for the job he'd previously accepted. Then it was back down to Dingle, the place he now calls home.

After one year at Benner's, Eric was offered the chance to head the kitchen at the soon-to-open Out of the Blue restaurant on the quay. While there was plenty of work to be done to establish a restaurant in what was then a fishmonger's shop, it wasn't yet a full-time operation, so he split his time between the pre-opening of OOTB and Murphy's Pub in Ballyferriter.

While working at OOTB – a place that both honed and steeled Eric's culinary chops – has been a professional success, the real boon in his life came on the personal side. In 2010, well into their rise on Irish food scene, a new manager, Neasa, came to work the front of house at OOTB. Eric and Neasa began dating early in the season of 2011. The couple now live on a small farm and raise much of the food that Eric uses in his farm-to-table menu.

A FARM TABLE

starter
Sorrel soup

main
Rabbit braised in cider and mustard

sides
Sauté potatoes
Sesame root vegetables

dessert
Baked chocolate bananas

cocktail suggestion
Bijou (page 251)

beverage suggestion
Semi-dry Normandy cider

I'm happy to say that Eric's braised rabbit dish was the first recipe in this book that I tested myself while my wife, Caryn, was away in Cork for a few days. I'm happy to say it because that meant I could finish every morsel of it myself. It's that good! If you've never tried rabbit, this is the perfect dish to give it a go. If you're not fond of it or can't find it, use the legs and thighs left over from the guinea fowl in Caroline Danaher's menu (page 192) and they'll be nearly as good. Fernando Lovisetto's potato gnocchi (page 163) rolling around in this cider sauce would be a lovely addition as well.

SORREL SOUP

Serves 6

15g / ½oz / 1 tbsp salted butter
1 shallot, finely chopped
2 bunches of sorrel, washed (stems peeled if thick) and all roughly chopped
400g / 14oz potatoes, peeled and finely diced
700ml / 1¼ pints / 2¾ cups + 2 tbsp water
250ml / 9fl oz / 1 cup cream
salt and ground white pepper

In a medium-sized pot over medium–low heat, melt butter and add shallot and a pinch of salt and cook, stirring, until soft. Add chopped sorrel and potatoes, toss to coat in butter. Add water, increase heat to medium–high and bring to a hard simmer. Reduce heat to medium and simmer until potatoes are soft, about 30 minutes.

Blend the soup until smooth, adding cream as you go. Correct the seasoning with salt and white pepper.

Chef's tip:
Sorrel is an arrow-shaped leaf and bright green in colour. The name is derived from the French word for 'sour'. The flavour is bright and lemony and, well ... sour, due to high concentrations of oxalic acid. It's a lovely herb, but you wouldn't want to eat it every day or in large quantities.

RABBIT BRAISED IN CIDER AND MUSTARD

Serves 6

2 x 800g / 1¾lb rabbits, cut up as noted

1 tbsp olive oil

15g / ½oz / 1 tbsp salted butter

2 shallots, finely chopped

1 red apple, peeled and grated

600ml / 1 pint / 2⅓ cups dry (hard) cider

200ml / 7fl oz / ¾ cup + 4 tsp cream

2 tbsp wholegrain mustard (or more to taste)

salt and freshly ground black pepper

Preheat the oven to 140°C / 280°F / gas mark 1.

The butcher can cut the rabbits for you, but if you're cutting them yourself, take off the back legs and cut in half, take front legs off at the shoulders, chop the body into three pieces.

Lightly season rabbit pieces with salt and pepper. Heat a large ovenproof casserole (Dutch oven) over medium–high heat, add oil and butter and brown the rabbit pieces in two batches so as not to crowd the pan.

Remove the rabbit to a warm plate, reduce heat to medium, add the shallots and apple and gently cook for 3 minutes.

Deglaze the pan with the cider and return rabbit to the pan. Increase heat to medium–high, bring to a hard simmer and reduce the heat to low or place in oven. Cook for about 1 hour 15 minutes, until rabbit is tender.

Remove the rabbit to a warm serving dish. Bring sauce to a simmer over medium heat, add cream and mustard. Reduce for about 10 minutes and season to taste. Pour sauce over rabbit pieces and serve.

SAUTÉ POTATOES

Serves 6

45g / 1½oz / 3 tbsp salted butter
1 tbsp olive oil
1.2kg / 2¾lb potatoes, peeled and cut into cubes
1 tbsp chopped fresh mixed herbs, such as parsley, rosemary, sage and marjoram
salt and freshly ground black pepper

In a large heavy-bottomed sauté pan or cast-iron pan set over a medium heat, melt half of the butter and the tablespoon of olive oil together. Add potatoes, toss to coat and lightly season.

Reduce heat to medium–low. Cook, tossing every so often, for about 20 minutes. Add more butter if needed. The potatoes are done when golden brown and crisp. Toss with the chopped fresh herbs and season to taste.

SESAME ROOT VEGETABLES

Serves 6

2 medium swedes (rutabaga), peeled and cut into 5mm x 5mm x 5cm / ¼in x ¼in x 2in batons
400g / 14oz young carrots, cut into batons
2 kohlrabi, peeled and cut into batons
45g / 1½oz / 3 tbsp butter
1 tbsp soy sauce
2 drops of toasted sesame oil
1 tbsp sesame seeds, toasted in a hot pan for 30 seconds or so
salt and freshly ground black pepper

Put the swede and carrot in a large pot of cold salted water over medium–high heat. Bring to a boil and add kohlrabi and half of the butter. Reduce heat to medium–low and simmer, partly covered, until vegetables are nearly tender, which should take 15–18 minutes. Remove lid and cook until veg are tender.

Drain and toss with remaining butter, soy sauce and sesame oil. Season with pepper only, as the soy should add enough saltiness. Garnish with toasted sesame seeds.

BAKED CHOCOLATE BANANAS

Serves 6

6 small bananas (Red Dwarf, Manzano, Niños or Lady Finger work well)
200g / 7oz dark chocolate, broken into small pieces
vanilla or chocolate ice cream, to serve

Preheat the oven to 190°C / 375°F / gas mark 5. Line a baking tray with non-stick baking paper. Place the unpeeled bananas on the lined tray. With a sharp paring knife, make a slit on the inside curve of the fruit to about three-quarters of the depth of the banana from about 1cm / ½in from the top to 1cm / ½in from the bottom to make a pocket for the chocolate. Stuff chocolate pieces into the pocket in the fruit to fill the pockets.

Bake in the oven for 12 minutes, until they are soft and the chocolate has melted. Serve with ice cream.

Chef's tip:
If you can't find fancy baby bananas, the smallest Cavendish (the most popular variety of cultivated banana in the world) you can find will work as well.

ONDŘEJ HASÍK

Fenton's

IF A TREE FALLS IN THE KITCHEN ...

Surf's up for a Czech chef transplanted to the Wild Atlantic Way

CHEF ONDŘEJ HASÍK opened his first restaurant, a bistro in a sporting venue in his home town of Jablonec, 80km outside Prague, when he was just nineteen years old, after a short career as a professional bowler.

His first aspiration was to follow many members of his family into the regional business of forestry. He attended college to pursue a degree in agriculture and forestry management at the same time as his twin sister headed off to hospitality training college.

He may have had no early ambitions to join the ranks of professional kitchens, but when Ondřej talks about the traditional Czech foods that his grandmother would cook, the sauces she would painstakingly make by hand (without the aid of modern culinary machinery) and the flavours he remembers around the family table, you can see that this man was born to cook.

Missing his twin and realising that felling trees wasn't a particularly sustainable career going forward, he switched colleges after a year to attend his sister's hospitality college and studied to become a chef. His particular interest in management and systems led Ondřej to placements in busy restaurants run by meticulous chefs with strong business heads.

After a positive experience in a busy, well-run Italian-themed restaurant and pizzeria, he headed to Italy to follow what he thought must be a national penchant for the food business, only to be discouraged by a shoddy facility run by unscrupulous management. Disillusioned, he followed his brother's advice and joined him in Kerry, Ireland, where his brother was sure Ondřej could find a place to put his culinary and managerial skills to good use. Chef's skills aside, Ondřej did not have a single word of the English language, which would have been quite a handicap in rural Ireland, so he worked as a hand for a couple of years for a dairy farmer who helped him learn the language.

It was a happy time, as he was living with his brother, working outdoors and learning a new language, and, as will happen, he met a lovely young woman too. With enough English to feel comfortable asking for a job, he moved to Dingle to be with his new girlfriend and get back into a kitchen.

Still shy about his language skills, he opted to ask for a washing-up job rather than a cooking job when he walked in the door of Fenton's. Having been forewarned of his visit by his girlfriend, who worked front of house, owner Patricia Fenton wouldn't hear of the talented young chef scrubbing pots. She put him to work in the busy restaurant to replace her head chef, who was retiring after eighteen years.

The first year at Fenton's wasn't easy for the chef, who hadn't even been born when the restaurant first opened its doors in 1985. Given the stresses of running a busy kitchen, establishing rapport with local purveyors and blending his style of cooking with decades-old tradition, the poor lad lost nearly 20kg in the first season and could often be seen in his kitchen during the overnight hours.

The beef, lamb, dairy and fish were overwhelming to the young chef, but not just because he was being spoiled for choice and quality. Don't forget that Ondřej left forestry because of an innate sense of sustainability and responsibility to the environment. That same accountability to the produce he cooks drives the young man to treat every steak and fish fillet, every rack of lamb and every bushel of shellfish with respect and reverence.

In short order, he has built a strong team, streamlined the systems of his kitchen and equipped it to the point where he's now more likely to be seen surfing a wave or tinkering on the campervan he built than stressing over the cost of the midnight oil he's burning.

The food Ondřej cooks is as solid as the trees he once studied. He brings an outsider's respect and fascination to his menu while creating the kind of food that people remember long after they've left our little corner of south-west Ireland.

This menu offers a wonderful blend of Ondřej's two homes: the one where he grew up and the one where he now lives and works. It's difficult to replicate the flavours of the wood-burning oven in which his grandmother cooked his favourite meals, but using a smoky barbecue grill to brown and sear the beef cheeks before braising them in porter and chocolate lends a hint of babička's cooking. Laura Walker's red cabbage (page 45) and Paul McPhillemy's spätzle (page 145) wouldn't be traditional accompaniments, but flavour trumps tradition almost every time in my book.

A TASTE OF THE FOREST

starter
Pumpkin soup with chilli and coriander

main
Smoky porter-braised beef cheeks

sides
Boiled Czech dumplings
Parsnip and apple purée

dessert
Grandmother's blueberry mint pie

cocktail suggestion
Marmalade Martini (page 259)

beverage suggestion
Beoir Chorca Dhuibhne Béal Bán, Porterhouse Herbrucker Lager or Crean's Lager

PUMPKIN SOUP WITH CHILLI AND CORIANDER

Serves 6

1 tbsp olive oil

15g / ½oz / 1 tbsp butter

1 red onion, finely chopped

3 garlic cloves, crushed

500g / 1lb 2oz potatoes, peeled and diced into 1cm / ½in cubes (Golden Wonders or Yukon Golds work well, both for flavour and texture)

1kg / 2¼lb pumpkin or butternut squash, peeled and diced into 5mm / ¼in cubes

1–2 fresh chillies, chopped

1 litre / 1¾ pints / 4 cups chicken stock or water

1 bunch of fresh coriander (cilantro), stems and all, chopped

120ml / 4fl oz / ½ cup cream

1 small handful (about ¼ cup) chives, finely chopped

salt and freshly ground black pepper

In a pot over medium heat melt olive oil and butter together. Add onion and a good pinch of salt. Cover and cook, stirring occasionally, until onion begins to soften but not brown, about 4 minutes. Add garlic and stir until fragrant, about 30 seconds. Add potatoes, pumpkin and chillies. Stir to coat.

Pour in stock (or water), bring to a simmer over medium–high heat and then reduce to medium–low. Cook until potatoes and pumpkin are tender, about 20 minutes.

Add coriander and purée using a hand-held blender until very smooth, adding more stock or water if needed. Pass through a fine-mesh sieve, stir in cream over medium–low heat and correct seasoning. Garnish with chives.

Chef's tip:
Kabocha, also known as Japanese pumpkin, works well in this soup too.

SMOKY PORTER-BRAISED BEEF CHEEKS

Serves 6

2–3 beef cheeks (about 900g / 2lb in total)
30g / 1oz / 2 tbsp butter, melted
coarse sea salt and freshly ground black pepper
30g / 1oz / 2 tbsp unsalted butter
8 shallots, peeled and halved
2 garlic cloves, sliced
4 sprigs of fresh thyme
350ml / 12fl oz / 1⅓ cups porter (Beoir Chorca Dhuibhne Carraig Dubh if possible, but any good stout or porter will do)
30g / 1oz good-quality dark chocolate (at least 80% cocoa solids), grated
750ml / 1¼ pints / 3 cups organic beef stock
1 tbsp blackcurrant jam
salt and freshly ground black pepper

Preheat the oven to 140°C / 280°F / gas mark 1. Preheat a barbecue grill (preferably charcoal or hardwood) to a very high heat.

Using a sharp knife, remove the sinew from the beef cheeks. Save any trimmings. Rub cheeks with melted butter and season well with coarse salt and cracked pepper. Sear well on very hot barbecue grill to get a deep crust on all sides. Remove to a wire rack over a rimmed baking tray and set aside.

In an ovenproof casserole (Dutch oven) over medium–high heat, melt the unsalted butter. Add beef trimmings and brown well. Remove and discard the trimmings.

Reduce heat to medium. Add shallots and fry until slightly browned, 8–10 minutes, stirring occasionally. Add sliced garlic and thyme sprigs. Stir to coat. Deglaze with porter and increase heat to medium–high. Bring to a boil and reduce for about 5 minutes. Remove from heat and stir in chocolate.

Add beef cheeks to the cooking liquid and add enough beef stock to just cover. Bring to a simmer, cover tightly with foil and then put the lid on. Place in preheated oven for 4–4½ hours, until very tender.

Let the dish cool for about 10 minutes before removing the beef to slice or shred as desired. Strain and defat the cooking liquid, reduce over medium heat. Stir in jam and correct seasoning.

Serve with dumplings on a warmed platter glazed with some of the cooking liquid and more served on the side.

BOILED CZECH DUMPLINGS

Serves 6–8

350ml / 12fl oz / 1⅓ cups milk
1 tsp caster (superfine) sugar
1 tsp dry (not instant) yeast
350g / 12oz / 3½ cups Wondra® instant flour – see note
1 tsp salt
1 egg, beaten

Note: The Wondra® instant flour in this recipe can be substituted by mixing 525g / 18½oz / 3½ cups) of plain (all-purpose) flour and 1¾ tsp of cornflour (cornstarch), sifting them together three times to aerate. Set aside 100g / 3½oz / ⅔ cup of the mixture for dusting.

In a small saucepan over low heat, warm milk to 37°C / 100°F. Remove from heat, stir in sugar and yeast. Set aside for 10 minutes to allow the yeast to activate.

In a medium-sized mixing bowl, mix flour and salt. Using a wooden spoon, stir in egg. Add the yeast and milk. Mix with wooden spoon until it begins to come together to form a dough.

Turn onto a lightly floured surface and knead until dough is no longer sticky and forms a ball.

Return to the bowl, dust lightly with flour and cover with a clean, warm, damp tea towel. Let rise in a warm spot for 2 hours.

Turn the dough onto a lightly floured board and divide into three equal portions. Gently form each portion into a cigar-shaped loaf about 15cm / 6in long. Cover with a clean, warm, damp tea towel to rise while you prepare the cooking water.

In a large stockpot, bring plenty of well-salted water to a boil. Add one dumpling loaf to boiling water and cover. Reduce heat to medium to maintain a gentle boil. Be careful, as the dissolved protein in the flour may cause the water to foam and boil over. Cook, covered, for 10 minutes. Gently turn the loaf over in the water to cook the second side an additional 10 minutes, again maintaining a gentle boil.

Remove the dumpling to a cutting board carefully so not to deflate. Prick with a fork in several places to release steam. Cook and cool remaining dumplings in the same manner.

These dumplings would traditionally be cut into slices 1–2cm / ½–¾in thick using a thread, but a serrated knife works well also. Serve alongside the braised beef cheeks and top with sauce.

PARSNIP AND APPLE PURÉE

Serves 6

750g / 1lb 10oz parsnips, peeled and cut into 2.5cm / 1in chunks
250g / 9oz celeriac, peeled and cut into 2.5cm / 1in chunks
2 Bramley cooking apples, peeled, cored and cut into 2.5cm / 1in chunks
30g / 1oz / 2 tbsp butter
60ml / 2fl oz / ¼ cup milk
salt and ground white pepper

Bring a large pan of salted water to a boil over high heat. Add vegetables and apples to the water. Bring to a simmer and reduce heat to medium to keep at just a simmer. Cook for about 12 minutes, until parsnips and celeriac are tender. Drain the water, cover with a clean tea towel and return to low heat to dry for 2–3 minutes.

Place the vegetables and apple in the bowl of a food processor (you may need to do this in two batches) with the butter, a little milk and some salt and white pepper. Process until smooth (you could also mash well by hand, if you like). Thin with additional milk as needed and correct seasoning.

Chef's tip:
Celeriac is a bulbous root of a particular kind of celery plant. Its surface is usually gnarled and nearly impossible to peel with a vegetable peeler. Use a chef's knife to cut away the outer peel and any roots still attached. Its flavour is warm and nutty with a hint of celery's salty edge.

GRANDMOTHER'S BLUEBERRY MINT PIE

Serves 6–8

For the pastry:
315g / 11oz / 2 cups + 2 tbsp plain (all-purpose) flour
10g / ¼oz / 2 tsp baking powder pinch of salt
1 tbsp caster (superfine) sugar
240g / 8½oz / 1 cup + 1 tbsp unsalted butter, chilled and cut into 16 pieces
100ml / 3½fl oz / ⅓ cup + 4 tsp ice water

For the filling:
250g / 9oz / 1 cup cottage cheese
1 bunch of fresh mint, leaves picked and chopped
3 tbsp granulated sugar
1 tbsp lemon juice
1 egg, separated
150g / 5¼oz / 1 cup blueberries
1 tsp caster (superfine) sugar

In a large mixing bowl, sift dry ingredients together. Place in the bowl of a food processer and add butter. Pulse four or five times, scrape down and pulse a few more times until the mixture looks like coarse meal. Scrape back into mixing bowl.

Using a rubber spatula, gently fold in enough ice water to make a moderately soft dough. Do not overmix. Wrap in cling film and refrigerate for 1 hour.

Preheat the oven to 170°C / 340°F / gas mark 3.

To make the filling, fold cottage cheese, mint, sugar, lemon juice and egg yolk together in a medium-sized bowl until well mixed. Set aside.

Roll out the pie dough to 3mm / ⅛in thickness and gently place into a 23cm / 9in pie plate. Fill the pie crust with the cottage cheese mixture and top with blueberries.

Whip egg white to soft peaks. Add caster sugar and continue to whip until medium-firm. Top the centre of the pie with this meringue, leaving several centimetres (a couple of inches) of the blueberries exposed.

Place in oven and bake for 20 minutes without opening the door. If meringue needs more time to set (and it should not brown), reduce heat to 140°C / 280°F / gas mark 1 for an additional 10 minutes. Best served warm.

BRIAN HEATON
Castlewood House

A CASTLE COURTSHIP

*Brian Heaton's (pictured here with his wife, Helen)
work kitchen is also the family kitchen*

THESE DAYS not many people can say that they met and fell in love with their spouse at a castle. But Brian Heaton, a handsome man with a devilish glint in his eye, is one who can. The Limerick man was working at Ashford Castle in Cong, County Mayo – as was his now wife, Helen – in the early 1990s. Today they own and run an award-winning guesthouse, Castlewood House, here in Dingle.

Brian worked his way through university, where he was studying engineering, by working as a barman at a busy local pub in the late 1980s. 'It was a time when everybody was in the pubs all hours of the day and night,' he recalls. 'And by everybody, I mean socially, economically – politicians, shop owners, tradesman and chancers … everybody. Back in the day, a pint was the great leveller.' It was a good way to lay the foundation for a long career in the hospitality industry.

A few years into his studies, Brian knew that engineering wasn't for him, but he stuck it out and received his degree and qualification. The hospitality bug had bitten when the owner of the pub took an extended holiday and left Brian in charge of the house, so he decided to draft his new career aspirations on this new plane. One summer he snared a position as room service waiter at Dromoland Castle in County Clare.

Never having had any experience in a professional kitchen, Brian was drawn to the camaraderie, the breadth of knowledge required and the passion that the men and women in this storied kitchen shared. It didn't hurt, of course, that the friends Brian was making in the kitchen could also make sure he got a taste of what the kitchen was serving to the paying guests rather than what was on offer in the employees' canteen.

Brian's appreciation of good food came from the cooking of his mother and especially his grandmother, who was raised in northern France. The way his granny cooked Sunday lunch with the same ingredients that everyone else in the neighbourhood had access to set his early food experiences apart from most of his friends. Once he began spending time – including his breaks and off-hours – around the exotic ingredients and the skilled hands cooking those foods at Dromoland, he was hooked.

The managing director of Dromoland and Ashford Castles offered to sponsor Brian through a rigorous hotel management course where students completed class work in about one quarter of the time allotted to traditional students while also giving them extensive practical experience in all aspects of hotel management. But no matter which department he was assigned to, Brian's eyes were always on the kitchen and his heart was beginning to wander in that direction as well.

The last two years of the curriculum was when a young Louth woman, Helen, came to work at Ashford as part of her own training programme, and Brian's world was set spinning.

Beginning his career in Dublin as the duty manager of a well-known hotel, Brian steadily worked his way up in the business and he married Helen in 2000, who by then was working in Dundalk, County Louth. The commute was hell, so he left the hotel world and began managing in the cinema world, from large movie theatres to a film distribution company, but the couple's dream was to open a little guesthouse somewhere nice and put down business and family roots.

After a few close calls in other parts of the country, they settled on the idea of moving to Dingle, where Brian's parents had moved and started a successful inn. The couple's purpose-built B&B has ticked all the boxes for travellers and awards since they opened in 2005.

Though Brian has never trained as a professional chef, his passion for and experience in the food and beverage side of hotels made him a natural for taking over the kitchen for breakfast. His unique use of savoury spices with fruits, his willingness to go the extra mile to stretch a guest's expectations of what an 'Irish' breakfast might be and the passion of a convert for local Dingle (and Kerry) ingredients would make his French granny proud ... and his Irish mammy as well.

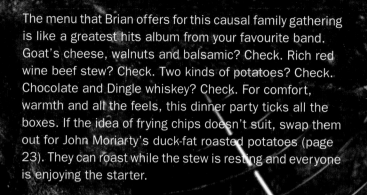

The menu that Brian offers for this causal family gathering is like a greatest hits album from your favourite band. Goat's cheese, walnuts and balsamic? Check. Rich red wine beef stew? Check. Two kinds of potatoes? Check. Chocolate and Dingle whiskey? Check. For comfort, warmth and all the feels, this dinner party ticks all the boxes. If the idea of frying chips doesn't suit, swap them out for John Moriarty's duck-fat roasted potatoes (page 23). They can roast while the stew is resting and everyone is enjoying the starter.

FAMILY FAVOURITES

starter
Goat's cheese and walnut salad
with balsamic dressing

main
Beef stew with red wine

sides
Buttered champ
Duck-fat chips and vinegar

dessert
Helen's decadent Dingle whiskey
chocolate torte

cocktail suggestion
Dingle French Martini or Pineapple
Ginger Fizz (pages 254 and 264)

wine suggestion
Mercurey

GOAT'S CHEESE AND WALNUT SALAD WITH BALSAMIC DRESSING

Serves 6

250g / 9oz beetroot, cooked in salted water until tender, cooled and peeled
4 tbsp olive oil
3 tbsp balsamic vinegar
200g / 7oz green beans, trimmed
150g / 5¼oz mixed salad leaves
½ cucumber, peeled into ribbons
100g / 3½oz goat's cheese log, halved horizontally
50g / 1¾oz / ½ cup walnut halves, toasted and roughly chopped
salt and freshly ground black pepper

Preheat the oven to 200°C / 400°F / gas mark 6.

Rub beetroot with 1 tablespoon of the oil and 1 tablespoon of the vinegar and season well. Roast for 8–10 minutes, until sticky. Remove and set aside for additional cooking with beans.

Bring a large pot of heavily salted water to a boil. Add the green beans and cook for 1 minute, then drain. Toss with the beetroot and roast for a further 5 minutes.

Make the dressing by combining the remaining oil and vinegar in a small bowl and season well. Put the mixed leaves and cucumber in a bowl and toss together with a little dressing.

Dip the cut sides of both cheese halves in the chopped toasted walnuts so the tops are covered, then pop in the roasting tin with the beetroot and green beans for a few minutes, to soften.

Pile the salad greens on a large serving platter, Arrange roasted beetroot and beans around the greens, place cheese pieces on top, drizzled with remaining dressing and season with salt and pepper.

Chef's tip:
Once you see how lovely the cucumber ribbons come out in this recipe, you'll use your vegetable peeler to cut loads of veg for salads. Ribbons of carrot and parsnip, lightly boiled, can even substitute for noodles.

BEEF STEW WITH RED WINE

Serves 6

1kg / 2¼lb best-quality stewing beef, cut into bite-sized pieces

50g / 1¾oz / ⅓ cup plain (all-purpose) flour

60ml / 2fl oz / ¼ cup Irish rapeseed oil

60g / 2oz / 4 tbsp butter

2 onions, diced medium

2 tsp tomato purée (paste)

250ml / 9fl oz / 1 cup red wine (I'd use a good Pinot Noir, particularly if serving with Mercurey)

500ml / 18fl oz / 2 cups beef stock

6 young carrots, cut in half lengthwise and then into slices 2cm / ¾in thick

1 punnet (basket) of mushrooms, sliced in half

1 herb bouquet (6 parsley sprigs, 2 thyme sprigs and 1 rosemary sprig, tied together)

1 fresh bay leaf

salt and freshly ground black pepper

Preheat the oven to 160°C / 320°F / gas mark 3.

Place the flour in a bowl and season heavily with salt and pepper. Add beef and toss to coat well. Shake off excess flour and set aside.

In a large ovenproof casserole (Dutch oven) over a low heat, melt half of the butter with 2 tablespoons of the oil. Add onions with a pinch of salt and cook until soft and medium brown, about 45 minutes. Stir in the remaining butter and oil.

Increase heat to medium–high and add beef. Cook, stirring once in a while, until meat has browned. Add tomato purée and cook for 30 seconds. Add red wine and deglaze. Add stock and bring to a boil. Add carrots, mushrooms, herb bouquet and bay leaf.

Cover and place in oven for 1½–2 hours, until meat is tender. Check regularly to ensure that the stock has not reduced too much. Top up with a little water or more stock if needed.

Remove herb bouquet and bay leaf. Season to taste and serve with buttered champ.

Chef's tip:
When tying your herb bouquet, leave an extra 3 or 4 inches of string at the end. This way you can leave the tail end hanging out of the pot, making it easier to pull out when the stew is finished.

BUTTERED CHAMP

Serves 6–8

12 medium potatoes, unpeeled and scrubbed well
100ml / 3½fl oz / ⅓ cup + 4 tsp cream
60g / 2oz / 4 tbsp butter
6 spring onions (scallions), thinly sliced
salt and freshly ground black pepper

Place potatoes in a large pot of salted cold water. Bring to a boil over medium–high heat. Reduce heat to medium–low and simmer until skins begin to break and potatoes are nearly tender, about 30 minutes. Turn off heat.

Drain, return the pot to the burner that was just turned off. Cover pot with a clean dry tea towel to absorb steam, place lid on top and leave for 10 minutes.

In a small saucepan, heat cream and half of the butter over medium–low heat until butter is melted and cream is hot.

Peel potatoes, using the towel to hold them, as they'll be hot. Mash using a food mill or a ricer, or mash by hand. Fold in the cream and butter mixture.

Season with salt and pepper to taste, adding more butter if desired – the more butter, the better! Fold in the sliced spring onions and serve.

DUCK-FAT CHIPS AND VINEGAR

Serves 6–8

1kg / 2¼lb potatoes (Queens, Golden Wonders or Yukon Golds work well)
2 litres / 3½ pints / 8 cups melted duck fat (see note)
dark malt vinegar, to taste
salt and freshly ground black pepper

Note: Not everyone has access to this quantity of duck fat. At a minimum, use 500ml / 18fl oz / 2 cups of duck fat and the remaining 1.5 litres / 2½ pints / 6 cups can be peanut oil or good-quality vegetable oil. The more duck fat there is in the mix, the better.

Wash, peel and cut the potatoes (along the longest line) into three equal slices, then turn 90° and cut another three equal slices. You'll now have nine large chips per potato (if these chips will be larger than 2cm / ¾in because you are using bigger potatoes, make four slices per side). Place chips into a large bowl, cover with cold water by 5cm / 2in, and then cover with ice cubes. Refrigerate for at least 30 minutes and up to 2 hours.

Set a heavy-bottomed 5-litre / 8¾-pint casserole (Dutch oven) fitted with a clip-on deep-frying thermometer over a medium–low heat. Add the duck fat (or fat and oil mixture) and heat to 150–160°C / 300–320°F. Make sure you have at least 7.5cm / 3in of room at the top of the casserole, as the chips will cause the fat to bubble.

Pour off the ice and water from the potatoes. Wrap potatoes in a clean tea towel and thoroughly pat them dry (you may need more than one towel).

Increase the heat to medium–high and add one or two handfuls of chips to the hot fat. Fry, stirring with a slotted spoon, until the wedges go limp and turn light gold, about 10 minutes.

Use the slotted spoon to transfer the chips to a wire cooling rack set over a rimmed baking tray to drain and cool. Let rest at least 10 minutes or up to 2 hours.

To serve, reheat the oil to 180°C / 350°F over a medium–high heat. Line the wire cooling rack with a triple-thick layer of kitchen paper (paper towels).

Increase the heat to high. Using the slotted spoon, transfer half of the potatoes to the hot fat. Stir the potatoes in the fat every once in a while until they reach a nice medium-brown colour and have puffed up a little, 8–10 minutes (lower the heat to medium–high if the temperature goes above 185°C / 365°F).

HELEN'S DECADENT DINGLE WHISKEY CHOCOLATE TORTE

Serves 6–8

110g / 4oz butter, plus extra for greasing

150g / 5¼oz dark chocolate (70–80% cocoa solids), chopped

60g / 2oz / ⅓ cup caster sugar

30g / 1oz / 3½ tbsp plain (all-purpose) flour

pinch of salt

3 eggs

2 tbsp Dingle whiskey

50g / 1¾oz / ⅓ cup dark brown sugar

250ml / 9fl oz / 1 cup cream, whipped, to serve

Preheat the oven to 180°C / 350°F / gas mark 4. Butter a 20cm / 8in round and 5cm / 2in deep cake tin very well.

Melt butter in a saucepan over a medium heat, allowing to sizzle and get quite hot. Remove from heat, add chocolate and whisk until smooth. Set aside to cool a little.

In a bowl sift together sugar, flour and salt. Add eggs and whiskey. Whisk until smooth.

Stir the brown sugar into the cooled chocolate mixture. Pour chocolate mixture into the flour mixture and stir.

Pour the batter into the greased tin. Bake in the middle of the oven for 25 minutes, remove and allow to cool on a wire rack.

Unmould the torte onto a cake stand and serve in slices with whipped cream.

MIKE HAYES

Dingle Supper Club

HIRED GUN

'Relaxing' in Mitchum's Bar,
Mike Hayes demonstrates
that not all chef's work is in
the kitchen

MIKE HAYES'S UNCLE, who had been working for years as a chef on oil rigs off the north coast of Scotland, gave him his first set of chef's whites when he headed to culinary school in the late 1990s. Looking at the path that Mike's career has taken him on, it seems fitting that a man doing yeoman's work, where food might be the only pleasure and comfort of the workers for weeks on end, would start him off on his journey.

Though food wasn't a major part of Mike's childhood in Limerick city, he does remember the days of *Ready Steady Cook* and the split in loyalty in his house when chef Ainsley Harriott took over from Fern Britton.

During his professional placements for his coursework at the Limerick Institute of Technology, he was put through his paces in the five-star kitchen of the Park Hotel in Kenmare. Head down with eyes and ears wide open (and mouth shut) is the way good apprentice chefs have learned the trade down through the generations. While Mike's eyes were opening to the food world beyond the small cafés and pubs he'd worked in before school, they also spotted young Collette waiting tables at the hotel and the spark was struck.

Collette was working her way through school in Cork. The couple met up again the following season when Mike went back for his second placement. He won't confirm or deny that it was because she was from the area and scheduled to be working there again, but they've been a couple ever since.

After a year of chasing the sunrises from Thailand to Australia to New Zealand and across America, the couple returned to help open the Cliff House Hotel in Waterford.

The list of hotels and restaurants in which Mike chose to further his experience and reputation reads like a who's who of famed kitchens. From Relais & Châteaux to Michelin Bib Gourmands positions of sous chef to first chef and head chef, he eventually became head of a five-star kitchen in a Killarney hotel, but with a baby on the way.

As you might imagine, the workload of a chef at the top of the hotel game is not conducive to what many would consider a normal family life. Knowing this, Mike stepped down from his role as chef and, taking his knowledge of how kitchens work and what chefs need, worked for two years as the representative of one of Ireland's best-known speciality food suppliers to the catering industry. His reputation as a successful head chef opened many kitchen doors to him, and during that time he heard many chefs complaining that they couldn't get qualified staff for weddings and other special functions. Thus, ChefHire.ie was born.

Mike's one-man outfit helping hotels with weddings quickly grew into a staff of five chefs, with scheduling and administrative support from Collette. Most people don't know that their wedding or special event at many of Kerry's finest hotels may actually be headed up by the chefs for hire that Mike has assembled. They are regular figures here in Dingle, running their pop-up restaurant out of Milltown House in the off-season and catering meals for the Dingle Supper Club and countless tours that come through the town.

Mike finds working in Dingle refreshing and quite different from any other part of Kerry. 'It's really like a county of its own down here,' he told me. 'The people are broader-minded about food. They're willing to try new things and they expect the restaurants to challenge them, and they don't suffer less than top quality.'

When Mike gets the chance to relax with his family and friends, he likes to have 80% of the work done before anyone walks in the door. 'I've spent too much time behind the kitchen doors to do that for a party,' he says. His menu affords the chef of the house the same relaxing evening as the guests.

FIVE-STAR COMFORT FOOD

starter
Cured salmon with wasabi, fennel, cucumber and watercress

main
Dingle lamb shepherd's pie with smoked Gubbeen cheese

dessert
Lemon posset

cocktail suggestion
Gin & Juice Punch (page 256)

wine suggestion
Grenache or Porterhouse Oyster Stout

This menu is another example of how doing a bit of work a few days in advance of your party can free you up to enjoy the evening. Traditionally, shepherd's pie was a dish made with the leftovers from a Sunday roast. Here, Mike slow-braises a lamb shoulder, which is even more flavourful than the leg, and uses that for his pie. Sublime! Eric Maillard's sorrel soup (page 201) would pair well with the cured salmon starter and Stella Doyle's salsa verde (page 28) is an excellent condiment for the lamb.

CURED SALMON WITH WASABI, FENNEL, CUCUMBER AND WATERCRESS

Serves 6–8

50g / 1¾oz / 3 tbsp fine sea salt

50g / 1¾oz / ¼ cup caster (superfine) sugar

1 lemon, zested

1 bunch of fresh coriander (cilantro)

1 x 600g / 1lb 5oz salmon fillet, skinned and all pin bones removed

For the lime mayonnaise:

2 tbsp mayonnaise

1 lime, juiced

wasabi paste

For the salad:

1 bunch of baby fennel herb

1 bunch of watercress

1 cucumber, peeled, cut in half lengthwise and seeded

Chef's tip:
While prepared wasabi paste – often in a tube – can be purchased, I prefer to use powdered wasabi as the flavour is much brighter. Simply mix the powder in a teacup with a few drops of water at a time until it just comes together as a paste. Turn the cup over on a cutting board for 2–3 minutes and the paste ready to use.

DAY 1

Mix salt, sugar, lemon zest and coriander in a food processor and pulse until coriander is cut fine. Rub the fish with this curing mixture (a little bit less of it on the thinnest part of the tail end), double wrap with cling film, place on a rimmed baking tray, put a second tray on top and weigh it down (a few cans of vegetables will do). Place in refrigerator for 24 hours.

DAY 2

Rinse the fish thoroughly and pat dry.

Mix the mayo, lime juice and a touch of wasabi. Pick the fennel and watercress leaves. Cut the cucumber into half-moon chunks.

To assemble, slice the salmon and decorate plate with the fennel and watercress leaves, cucumber chunks and wasabi. Serve the lime mayonnaise on the side.

DINGLE LAMB SHEPHERD'S PIE WITH SMOKED GUBBEEN CHEESE

Serves 6–8

1 lamb shoulder, boneless

3 tbsp Irish rapeseed oil

30g / 1oz / 2 tbsp butter

1 carrot, cut into large chunks

1 fennel bulb, sliced

1 onion, diced

1 head of garlic, cloves peeled and halved

150ml / 5¼fl oz / ⅔ cup red wine

3 x 400g / 14oz cans of chopped tomatoes

2 litres / 3½ pints / 8 cups lamb stock

1 bay leaf

1 sprig of fresh rosemary

4 tsp HP brown sauce

100g / 3½oz / ¾ cup petits pois (baby peas)

salt and freshly ground black pepper

For the mashed potato topping:

12 large potatoes (preferably Maris Piper, but any good floury potato will do), peeled and quartered

45g / 1½oz / 3 tbsp butter

60ml / 2fl oz / ¼ cup cream

salt and freshly ground black pepper

200g / 7oz smoked Gubbeen cheese (or your favourite smoked Cheddar), grated

Chef's tip:
Have your butcher bone the shoulder, but keep the bones. They'll be useful for making stock for stews and soups as well as other braised dishes.

Preheat the oven to 180°C / 350°F / gas mark 4.

Season lamb very well. Heat a large casserole (Dutch oven) over a medium–high heat. Add oil and heat until shimmering. Brown the lamb very well on both sides. Remove and set aside.

Reduce heat to medium, add butter to the same pot and carrot, fennel, onion and garlic. Cook, stirring often, until browned a little. Deglaze with the wine and scrape up the browned bits. Add tomatoes, cook for 3 minutes and then add lamb stock and herbs.

Increase heat to high and bring to a boil. Place the lamb back into the pot, cover tightly with foil. Put the covered pot into the oven for 30 minutes, then reduce to 120°C / 250°F / gas mark ½ for 3 hours. Remove the lamb from the pot and allow to cool slightly. Remove bay leaf and separate the fat from the cooking liquid and vegetables.

Increase the oven temperature to 200°C / 400°F / gas mark 6.

While lamb is cooling, place potatoes in a steamer basket over 10cm / 4in of boiling salted water. Steam potatoes for about 8 minutes. Rinse to remove some of the starch and then return to steam until cooked.

In a small saucepan over medium heat, heat the butter and cream together.

Mash the potatoes by hand or using a food mill. Thin with cream and butter. Season to taste, put into a large piping bag with a star tip ready to pipe over the meat or you can simply spoon the potatoes on top of the pie.

Using a hand-held blender, blitz the reserved cooking liquid and vegetables. Season to taste.

When the lamb has cooled down enough to handle, pull it apart into large pieces and add to the puréed cooking liquid and stir in HP sauce. Ladle lamb and sauce into an ovenproof dish, top with peas. Pipe (or spoon) the potatoes on top of the dish to completely cover. Top with the grated cheese and bake in the pre-heated oven for 10–15 minutes, until nicely browned.

LEMON POSSET

Serves 6

2 sheets of gelatine
680ml / 23fl oz / 2¾ cups cream
150g / 5¼oz / ¾ cup caster (superfine) sugar
3 lemons, zested and juiced, plus extra zest to decorate

Soak the gelatine in cold water.

In a medium-sized non-reactive saucepan over medium heat, bring the cream and sugar to a simmer. Squeeze the gelatine and add to the cream with the lemon zest and juice. Stir to dissolve and strain into a measuring jug.

Pour into six serving glasses – beautiful wine glasses work nicely. Chill for at least 12 hours or overnight. Decorate with additional lemon zest.

Chef's tip:
The posset we eat today is nothing like the original dish. Originating in the Middle Ages, it was a drink made of milk, curdled with ale or wine and usually used medicinally. Today's posset is more mousse-like and akin to syllabub.

JULIAN WYATT
Ceann Sibéal Hotel

SURE, WHY DON'T YOU CHANCE IT?

Labradors Frog and Mole are ready to retrieve whatever Julian hunts down

LITTLE ABOUT THE WAY that Julian Wyatt, chef at Ceann Sibéal Hotel, came to prominence in the food world was direct or typical. I refer to him as a Cork man even though he was born in Cheltenham, spent three of his first sixteen years in France and moved around the UK with his family for the other thirteen, which all helped to lay the broad platform for the young man's life, let alone his career.

Leaving school in England at the age of sixteen, he moved to his father's family home place in north Cork, where he'd spent most holidays growing up. In need of a job and already having a full-blown passion for food, he saw a job posting for a commis chef at the prestigious Longueville House. Not knowing what a commis chef was, he asked his father, who explained that it would be an entry-level position, one that usually requires formal training and certainly would in a place like Longueville House. 'Sure, why don't you chance it?' his father said, and that's just what Julian did.

Offered a position doing the washing-up, he told the head chef that he'd prefer the commis job working with food. He was given a one-day trial and was hired on the spot. Not bad for a sixteen-year-old with no restaurant experience!

With an adaptability suited for the business, Julian bounced around in the off-season, taking advantage of his employer's contacts, and was made chef de partie in short order and got his first head chef job in the UK before he was twenty-one. Then

he was headhunted to run the kitchens of a Scottish hotel outside Glasgow, where he took the food from strength to strength, racking up awards and accolades, but he knew that he was reaching the limits of his ability and drive.

Moving to the Champagne-Ardenne region of France, he took a job as premier commis – very near where he had started in the business – at a small hotel. Not speaking the language beyond what chefs call 'kitchen French', he was behind the eight ball from the beginning. It was tough work, probably the hardest work he'd done up to that point in his life, but he learned quickly and was soon rising up the culinary ladder again. 'I wouldn't do it again and I wouldn't advise it either,' Julian told me over an off-season pint in Dingle, 'but I learned an awful lot and it made me the chef that I am today.'

He moved from the hotel to a restaurant and then to a high-quality catering firm (holder of the coveted Un des Meilleurs Ouvriers de France classification), where he was once again head chef, before taking over another restaurant.

Every year he would visit his uncle's holiday home on the Dingle Peninsula in the off-season to keep in touch with his Irish roots and relax. He brought along the Frenchwoman he'd fallen in love with (and eventually married) and she, too, felt a strong connection with the area.

When a deal to purchase his own restaurant near their village fell through, leaving him in a tricky position, he heard his father's words again, this time via his uncle: 'Sure, why don't you chance it?' The couple came with their young son to stay in the uncle's place while looking for chef's work in Dingle.

The transition from the way the French cook their food to the way people in west Kerry expect their meals to be prepared was quite difficult. Working mostly with fish in Dingle versus making terrines, pâté and hours-long preparations of meats was a bit of a change after eleven years of French country cooking. But as I heard time and time again while interviewing chefs in Dingle, the ingredients dictate that we do as little to them as possible in order for their goodness to shine through.

He always wanted to come back to Ireland to work, and even though he always envisioned that he and his family might move to Cork, Dingle has offered Julian a unique opportunity. We look forward to seeing how the landscape of west Kerry food changes with Julian Wyatt hoeing his row in our communal culinary garden.

Sitting in O'Flaherty's Pub in Dingle discussing this menu with Julian, my excitement was so obvious that he resolved to make it and have me over the following week. This, like Paul McPhillemy's menu (page 140), is a version of a chef's restaurant food brought home for a party. There are many steps to preparing this menu as a whole, but it also breaks down well as courses to add to your own repertoire of dinner menus at home. The rösti potato could be replaced with John Ryan's baked sweet potato wedges (page 11) if you like, and by adding more than a splash of champagne, Julian's cranberry sorbet could be served as a lovely cocktail.

A HUNTER'S LUNCH

starter

Salade de gésiers de canard confit
(salad of confit duck gizzards)

main

Grilled quails with morel mushroom sauce and quail Scotch egg in a spinach nest

sides

Rösti potato

dessert

Dingle gin and cranberry sorbet with champagne

cocktail suggestion

The West Kerry Hedgerow (page 263)

wine suggestion

Côtes du Roussillon red

SALADE DE GÉSIERS DE CANARD CONFIT (SALAD OF CONFIT DUCK GIZZARDS)

Serves 6

700g / 1lb 9oz fresh duck or chicken gizzards
2 fresh bay leaves, torn into pieces
500g / 1lb 2oz duck fat
3 heads of Belgian endive
12 radishes, thinly sliced
1 tbsp pine nuts, toasted
2 shallots, finely chopped
3 tbsp raspberry vinegar, plus a little extra
2 tbsp extra virgin olive oil
1 tbsp truffle oil
fresh chives
salt and freshly ground black pepper

Chef's tip:
Confit is from the French word 'confire' which literally means 'to preserve'. Salting and simmering in fat cures and cooks the meat. Cooling and storing the meat in fat then creates a barrier to the air, and thus was a perfect method of preserving meats for the winter months. Confit was the original 'potted meat' as it was cooked and stored in earthenware pots.

DAY 1

Clean and dry gizzards, removing any membrane. Season heavily with salt, pepper and bay leaves. Place in container, cover and marinate overnight in the refrigerator.

DAY 2

Preheat the oven to 150°C / 300°F / gas mark 2.

Rinse gizzards, pat dry and discard bay leaf pieces. Place in an ovenproof casserole (Dutch oven), cover with duck fat and bring to a gentle simmer over medium–low heat. Cover and place in oven for 2–2½ hours, until tender. Remove from heat, let cool in fat and refrigerate (in the fat) overnight.

DAY 3

Remove gizzards from fat and slice in half. Set aside.

Garnish six plates with endive spears, radish slices and a few pine nuts.

Make a dressing by placing shallots and 1 tablespoons of the raspberry vinegar in a small bowl. Slowly whisk in the olive oil and truffle oil. Season with salt and pepper.

In a large frying pan over medium–high heat, reheat gizzards, browning them a little on both sides. Deglaze the pan with remaining 2 tablespoons of raspberry vinegar.

Arrange warm gizzards on plate with salad and drizzle dressing over the endive and radishes. Spoon any pan juices over gizzards. Garnish with a few whole chives.

GRILLED QUAILS WITH MOREL MUSHROOM SAUCE AND QUAIL SCOTCH EGG IN A SPINACH NEST

Serves 6

12 quails
500ml / 18fl oz / 2 cups chicken stock
60ml / 2fl oz / ¼ cup olive oil
1 tsp fresh thyme leaves
300g / 10½oz baby spinach

For the Scotch eggs:
1 small duck breast
pinch of ground nutmeg
6 quail eggs
120g / 4¼oz / 1 cup plain (all-purpose) flour, seasoned with salt and pepper
1 egg, scrambled

60g / 2oz / 1 cup panko Japanese-style breadcrumbs
1 litre / 1¾ pints / 4 cups vegetable oil, for frying

For the morel mushroom sauce:
1 shallot, finely chopped
15g / ½oz / 1 tbsp butter
60g / 2oz fresh morel mushrooms (or 20g / ¾oz dried, soaked for 30 minutes in warm water and drained)
2 tbsp brandy
300ml / ½ pint / 1¼ cups cream
salt and freshly ground black pepper

Fillet the quail and debone the legs. Place bones in stock and simmer for 45 minutes. Marinate the quail fillets with olive oil, thyme, salt and pepper. Set aside.

To make the Scotch eggs, cut up the quail leg meat and duck breast. Pulse in food processor until the texture of mince. Season with salt, pepper and nutmeg.

Place quail eggs in boiling water for 2 minutes 35 seconds. Refresh in ice water, then peel.

Roll out the duck and quail mince between two layers of cling film. Divide into six equal portions and carefully wrap around the peeled quail eggs.

Preheat oil to 185°C / 365°F.

Roll coated eggs in flour, then egg wash and then breadcrumb. Deep-fry until golden brown. Drain on kitchen paper (paper towels).

To make the sauce, over medium–high heat, sauté shallot and morels in butter until mushrooms take on a bit of colour. Take off heat, add brandy and flambé. Return to heat and add stock, reduce by half, add cream, reduce. Correct the seasoning.

Wilt spinach in a hot pan with a little butter and water. Season with salt and pepper.

Chargrill or barbecue quail fillets to medium rare.

Serve with the morel sauce, wilted spinach nest and quail egg.

RÖSTI POTATO

Serves 6

4–5 potatoes, peeled and grated lengthwise
1 tsp cornflour (cornstarch)
salt and freshly ground black pepper
60g / 2oz / 4 tbsp butter

Place the grated potatoes in a large bowl, fill with cold water, and swirl to remove excess starch. Drain the potatoes in a colander. Working in two batches, wrap the potatoes in a clean tea towel, squeeze out the excess liquid and transfer the potatoes to a dry bowl. Sprinkle the cornflour, ½ teaspoon salt and ¼ teaspoon pepper over the potatoes and gently toss until thoroughly incorporated. Set aside.

Melt half of the butter in a frying pan over medium heat. Add the potato mixture and spread it into an even layer. Cover and cook for 6 minutes.

Uncover and use a spatula to press the potatoes down gently to form a compact, round cake. Continue to cook, uncovered, occasionally pressing on the potatoes to shape into a uniform round cake, until the bottom is deep golden brown, 4–5 minutes longer. Slide the rösti onto a large plate.

Melt the remaining butter in the frying pan. Invert the rösti onto a second plate and slide it back into the frying pan, browned side up. Continue to cook, uncovered, and occasionally pressing down on the cake, until the bottom is well browned, 5–7 minutes.

Remove the pan from the heat and allow the rösti to cool in the pan for 5 minutes. Slide the rösti onto a cutting board and cut into six wedges.

Chef's tip:
This potato dish takes some practice. Once you get the hang of it, you'll be making it for breakfast, lunch and dinner. Be patient, because it takes a good while to brown the potatoes as you're cooking the inner layers over low heat.

DINGLE GIN AND CRANBERRY SORBET WITH CHAMPAGNE

Serves 6

1 litre / 1¾ pints / 4 cups cranberry juice
1 lemon, juiced
100g / 3½oz / ½ cup caster (superfine) sugar
1 double shot of Dingle Original Gin
champagne, to serve
6 sprigs of fresh thyme, to serve

In a medium-sized saucepan over medium–high heat, place cranberry juice, lemon juice and sugar. Stir to dissolve and reduce by half. Remove from heat and cool completely.

Add gin and freeze in an ice cream machine or pour into a shallow glass baking dish and freeze, stirring often, for about 4 hours.

To serve, scoop sorbet into attractive glasses, add a splash of champagne around the sorbet and decorate with a sprig of thyme.

Chef's tip:
Cranberry juice 'drink' or 'cocktail' can be substituted in this sorbet, but if you can find 100 per cent cranberry juice, the dish will be brighter and fresher tasting.

LEE SIM

The Dingle Whiskey Distillery

THE BEST MEMORIES ARE FOOD MEMORIES

*The sign reads, 'I'm Outdoorsy
... I like to drink wine on patios!'
'Nuff said.*

A S THE CULINARY DIRECTOR of nine eateries in three countries, Yorkshire-born, Manchester-reared Lee Sim probably oversees more meals each day than all the other chefs in this book combined. Not being a classically trained chef, he's a bit shy about just how large his culinary reach is.

From an early age, Lee knew that flavour was important. Bold flavour equalled big experience. His mother worked in a jam factory in Manchester and would bring home samples of her work that Lee would pile on slices of bread and incorporate into simple baked goods even before he reached the age of ten.

He didn't see the food business as his career path early on. Attending college to study computer engineering, Lee, like many chefs in Dingle and the wider world, took odd jobs in the restaurant and pub trade to make ends meet and pay for a few pints down the pub while at college. But a passion was sparked.

After abandoning computer engineering, he found himself gaining on-the-job training as a brewer at a newly opened microbrewery pub. The early days of craft brewing in England were a tough nut to crack, with inexpensive beer on many suburban taps. Food offerings were seen as a way to keep the business afloat, so Lee jumped from the brewhouse into the kitchen to help save the foundering ship. He lived on site, so as he read up on recipes and trends in cookery books, food magazines and trade journals, he could run down to the kitchen at all hours to test out recipes and he was hooked.

When the brewing and kitchen crews headed to the Basque region of Spain to help another small brewpub open, San Sebastián and its surrounds made a deep and lasting impression on the team.

The head brewer of the pub asked Lee if he was up for the challenge of helping to open another new brewery/pub, this time in Dublin. That was the original Porterhouse, the first of its kind in Ireland, and Lee never looked back to the idea of computer engineering (or brewing, for that matter). By the time Porterhouse was ready to open a new pub in London, he had assumed the role of culinary director and Chef Lee Sim was baptised by fire.

Moving from an English-inspired brewpub, Lee then oversaw a project of passion in opening a series of new Port House tapas bars throughout Dublin. Melding his development and managerial skills, a love of Basque flavours and a new interest in Iberian wines, the concept, with a bit of tweaking to fit Irish service sensibilities, was a success from the start.

The Dingle connection comes in the form of the Dingle Whiskey Distillery, which opened its big door in December 2012. The distillery was opened by the Porterhouse founder, the late Oliver Hughes. Lee's culinary fingerprints are all over the catered events that take place at the distillery. From the annual Founding Fathers do to special events for international VIPs, Lee combines typical west Kerry subtleness with a sprinkle of his trademark bold flavours, giving his diners a chance to experience the fruits of his own travels. 'I travel to make memories,' Lee told me as we chatted in his development kitchen. 'My best memories are food memories.'

Lee encourages his two teenage children to try new things, experience new flavours and develop an international sensibility about food when they travel together. Whether his customers are eating an Irish beef burger in New York City, nibbling saffron-infused croquettes in D2 or queuing at the buffet for an event at the Dingle Whiskey Distillery, Lee's intention is to create memories – and food memories at that – for people experiencing his food.

Using local ingredients when possible, enhancing them with high-quality imported speciality products and offering them up in fun and relaxing atmospheres is how Lee Sim remembers his favourite meals, and it's what he hopes to bring to the experience of tourists and local diners, whether in Dingle, London or wherever his next kitchen might be.

Paella is one of those dishes that everyone but the Spanish thinks is an intricate and difficult meal to prepare. If we would only understand that it's the nation's barbecue-at-the-beach food, like ribs and bratwurst to Americans or sausages and chicken skewers to the Irish, maybe we'd make it more often. Lee's recipe for rabbit and prawn paella is perfect just as it is, but you can change it up with chicken and shrimp, quail and chorizo, or lobster and shellfish. Make it once and you'll be back to this deep culinary well time after time. Stella Doyle's mixed greens salad (page 30) would be a nice addition to this menu if you want to have some greens on your buffet.

SAN SEBASTIÁN MEMORIES

starters
Fresh Dingle crab mayonnaise
Pan de aceite (Spanish olive oil bread)

main
Paella of rabbit and Dingle Bay prawns

dessert
Tarte tatin with crème fraîche

cocktail suggestion
Limoncello Collins (page 258)

wine suggestion
Txakoli de Getaria DO from the Basque country

FRESH DINGLE CRAB MAYONNAISE

Serves 6

For the mayonnaise:

4 large egg yolks

2 tbsp + 2 tsp fresh lemon juice

½ tsp Dijon mustard

¼ tsp caster (superfine) sugar

¼ tsp fine sea salt

ground white pepper, to taste

300ml / ½ pint / 1¼ cups high-quality Irish rapeseed oil

60ml / 2fl oz / ¼ cup extra virgin olive oil

For the crab salad:

500g / 1lb 2oz cooked Dingle brown crabmeat (Dungeness or other crab could be substituted)

1 bunch of spring onions (scallions), finely chopped

300ml / ½ pint / 1¼ cups mayonnaise (reserve remaining mayonnaise in the refrigerator for up to three days)

2 tsp Dijon mustard

2 tbsp crème fraîche

½ lemon, juiced

coarse sea salt flakes

freshly ground black pepper

To make the mayonnaise, pulse the yolks, 2 tablespoons of the lemon juice, the mustard, sugar, salt and pepper in a food processor for about 10 seconds, until combined. With machine running, gradually add oils in slow, steady stream (process should take about a minute). Scrape down sides of bowl with rubber spatula and process 5–10 seconds longer. Adjust seasoning with additional salt, pepper and the remaining 2 teaspoons of lemon juice. Pulse two or three times after seasoning. Place in a clean container, cover and refrigerate for 1 hour before use.

To prepare the crab, place all the ingredients except the salt and pepper in a large mixing bowl and gently toss to combine. Season lightly with salt and add a good amount of pepper. Place into your chosen serving bowl, cover and refrigerate until 30 minutes before serving. Serve with warm pan de aceite.

Chef's tip: You can, of course, substitute commercial mayonnaise in this dish, but once you've tried it with homemade you may never buy the jarred stuff again.

PAN DE ACEITE (SPANISH OLIVE OIL BREAD)

Makes about 2 dozen pieces

2 sachets of dried yeast (not instant)
1 tsp caster (superfine) sugar
400ml / 14fl oz / 1⅔ cups lukewarm water
4 tsp extra virgin olive oil, plus more for brushing
500g / 1lb 2oz / 3⅓ cups strong white flour (bread flour)
10g / ¼oz / 2 tsp salt
coarse sea salt

Preheat the oven to 180°C / 350°F / gas mark 4.

In a medium bowl, combine yeast with sugar and half the water, stir and leave for 1 hour. Add remaining water and oil to the yeast and whisk together.

Sift flour and salt together in the bowl of a stand mixer fitted with a dough hook. Add yeast starter to the flour and mix on low speed for 10 minutes, until glossy and elastic. Cover with a clean, warm, damp tea towel and prove for 1 hour, until doubled in size.

Knock back the dough and divide into 30g / 1oz balls roughly 3cm / 1¼in across and then press into discs. Lay on a sheet of non-stick baking paper and brush with oil. Cover with another sheet of non-stick baking paper and allow to rise for 30 minutes.

Brush with more oil and sprinkle with coarse sea salt. Bake for 12–14 minutes, until golden.

PAELLA OF RABBIT AND DINGLE BAY PRAWNS

Serves 6

2 x 800g / 1¾lb rabbits, cut into pieces – see note

12 large Dingle Bay prawns or extra-large shrimp, shell and head on if possible

salt and freshly ground black pepper

olive oil

8 medium garlic cloves, finely chopped

1 red bell pepper, seeded and cut pole to pole into strips 1cm / ½in thick

500g / 1lb 2oz Spanish chorizo, sliced into coins 1cm / ½in thick

1 onion, finely chopped

1 x 400g / 14oz can of chopped tomatoes, drained, finely chopped and drained again

400g / 14oz / 2 cups Valencia rice

750ml / 1¼ pints / 3 cups warm chicken stock (3¼ cups if using a paella pan)

80ml / 3fl oz / ⅓ cup dry white wine (120ml / 4fl oz / ½ cup if using a paella pan)

½ tsp saffron threads, crumbled

1 fresh bay leaf

70g / 2½oz / ½ cup petits pois (baby peas)

1 tbsp roughly chopped fresh parsley

1 lemon, cut into 6 wedges, to serve

Preheat the oven to 180°C / 350°F / gas mark 4. Adjust rack to lower middle position in the oven.

Note: The butcher can cut the rabbits for you, but if you're cutting them yourself, take off the back legs and cut in half, take front legs off at the shoulders, chop the body into four pieces.

Season the rabbits well with salt and pepper. Set aside.

Toss prawns, ¼ teaspoon salt, ¼ teaspoon black pepper, 1 tablespoon oil and 1 teaspoon garlic in a medium bowl. Cover with plastic wrap and refrigerate until needed.

In a large casserole (Dutch oven) or a paella pan with a diameter of at least 35.5–38cm / 14–15in (no smaller) set over medium–high, heat 2 teaspoons oil until shimmering but not smoking. Add pepper strips and cook, stirring occasionally, until skin begins to blister and turn spotty black, 3–4 minutes. Transfer pepper to small plate and set aside.

Add 1 teaspoon oil to now-empty pan. Heat oil until shimmering but not smoking. Add rabbit pieces in single layer (this may take several batches) and cook, without moving pieces, until browned, about 3 minutes. Turn pieces and brown on second side, about 3 minutes longer. Transfer to medium bowl.

Reduce heat to medium and add chorizo to the pan. Cook, stirring frequently, until deeply browned and fat begins to render, 4–5 minutes. Transfer chorizo to bowl with rabbit and set aside.

Reduce heat to medium and add enough oil to the fat to equal 2 tablespoons in total (or take some out if there is too much). Heat until shimmering.

Add onion and cook, stirring frequently, until softened, about 3 minutes. Stir in remaining garlic and cook until fragrant, about 1 minute. Stir in tomatoes and cook until mixture begins to darken and thicken slightly, about 3 minutes. Stir in rice and cook until grains are well coated with tomato mixture, 1–2 minutes. Stir in stock, wine, saffron, bay leaf and a good pinch of salt.

Return rabbit and chorizo to pan, increase heat to medium–high and bring to boil, uncovered, stirring occasionally.

Cover the casserole (Dutch oven) or tightly cover the paella pan with foil and transfer to oven. Cook until rice has absorbed almost all liquid, about 15 minutes. Remove pot from oven (close oven door to retain heat). Uncover pot and lay prawns over rice, arrange bell pepper strips in pinwheel pattern and scatter peas over top. Cover the casserole again (or cover with foil again if using a paella pan) and return to oven. Cook until prawns are bright pink, 10–12 minutes.

Remove from the oven, uncover and set on the hob (stovetop) over a medium–high heat about 5 minutes (3 minutes for a paella pan), rotating the pot 180° after about 2 minutes (1½ minutes for a paella pan) for even browning of the bottom. Do not let burn.

Remove from heat, cover and let paella stand for about 5 minutes. Sprinkle with parsley, arrange lemon wedges and serve.

Chef's tip:
If you cannot find Valencia rice - a short-grained rice that absorbs liquid without breaking down - Arborio rice (the same rice used in risotto) can be used but the dish will be much creamier than normal paella.

TARTE TATIN WITH CRÈME FRAÎCHE

Serves 6–8

For the pastry:
110g / 4oz / 1 stick cold butter, cubed
175g / 6¼oz / 1 cup + 2 tbsp plain (all-purpose) flour
2 egg yolks
3 tbsp caster (superfine) sugar
ice water

For the filling:
75g / 2½oz / 5 tbsp butter
6 tbsp caster (superfine) sugar
7 Granny Smith apples, peeled, cored and cut into 6–7 wedges
crème fraîche, to serve

To make the pastry, in a large mixing bowl rub the butter and flour together until resembling breadcrumbs. Add egg yolks, sugar and 2–3 tablespoons of water. Mix into a ball. Wrap in cling film and refrigerate for 15–30 minutes.

Preheat the oven to 220°C / 430°F / gas mark 8.

To make the filling, melt the butter and sugar in a sauté pan over a medium heat. When syrupy and a deep golden brown, add the apples. Move them around in the sauce until they are roughly level.

Roll out the pastry to form a circle that will fit inside the pan. Lay the pastry over the apples and pat it down gently.

Place the pan in preheated oven, turn heat down to 200°C / 400°F / gas mark 6 and bake for 40 minutes, until the pastry is light brown and the juice is bubbling. Cool on a wire rack for 5 minutes.

Run a paring knife around the edge of the tart, place a serving plate on top and quickly flip over so that the crust is on the plate and the apples are on top. Serve with crème fraîche.

Chef's tip:
This dessert can also be served with ice cream. Rather than plain vanilla, why not try Rachael Boyle's crème fraîche ice cream (page 157)?

COCKTAILS
WITH THE DINGLE DISTILLERY

I offer these cocktail recipes using the premium products from our Dingle Whiskey Distillery. If you are not fortunate enough to live somewhere you can find Dingle Original Gin, Dingle Distillery vodka or Dingle whiskey, please use a premium replacement. You are, after all, emulating the menus of chefs who rarely get to entertain. When we play, we play with only the best.

Many of these recipes are for a batch of six cocktails. Pre-mix and have in an appropriate glass cocktail pitcher and allow your guests to help themselves. Some will be light on the pour and some a bit heavier. Either way, there will be plenty for everyone ... and maybe even an extra for the deserving chef of the night.

Please ensure that your guests have a safe way home after their evening with you – or have the spare rooms made up. Drink driving is never an option.

BIJOU

Makes 6 cocktails

250ml / 9fl oz / 1 cup Dingle Original Gin
80ml / 3fl oz / ⅓ cup sweet vermouth
80ml / 3fl oz / ⅓ cup Chartreuse
6 dashes orange bitters
ice
lemon peel cut with channel knife for garnish

In a cocktail pitcher, mix gin, vermouth, Chartreuse and bitters.
Fill a cocktail shaker with ice. Add a double measure of gin mixture and shake well.
Strain into cocktail (martini) glasses and garnish with lemon twist.

~~~~~~

BLACK VELVET

Makes 6–8 cocktails

1 bottle champagne (or prosecco, cava or sparkling wine of your choice)
3 bottles Porterhouse Plain Porter, Beoir Chorca Dhuibhne Carraig Dubh (or any stout you like)

Keep champagne and porter very cold in ice buckets.
Half-fill tall champagne flutes with champagne. Gently pour porter to fill the glass, being careful that it doesn't foam over.

~~~~~~

BLOOD ORANGE AND CAVA MIMOSA

(with 'virgin' option)
Makes 6 cocktails

180ml / 6fl oz / ¾ cup freshly squeezed blood orange juice
1 bottle Spanish cava
strawberries to garnish

Half-fill champagne flutes with juice. Top up with cava. Garnish with a strawberry.
If you're having this at brunch and it might be a bit early for some, as well as the likelihood that underaged guests will be in attendance, replace the cava with sparkling water and you have a lovely non-alcoholic substitute. Cheers!

BRAMBLE

Makes 6 cocktails

250ml / 9fl oz / 1 cup fresh lemon juice
250ml / 9fl oz / 1 cup gomme syrup (recipe on page 266)
500ml / 18fl oz / 2¼ cups Dingle Original Gin
80ml / 3fl oz / ⅓ cup crème de mure
1 lemon, sliced
1 punnet blackberries, washed
crushed ice

In a large glass pitcher, stir together lemon juice, syrup, Dingle Original Gin and crème de mure.
Add sliced lemon and half of the blackberries and stir gently.
Three-quarter fill lowball cocktail glass with crushed ice, pour Bramble into glass and garnish with blackberry.

CLASSIC DINGLE GIN TONIC

Makes 6 cocktails

300ml / ½ pint / 1¼ cups Dingle Original Gin
1 lemon, sliced
2 limes, one sliced, one wedged for garnish
ice cubes
6 x 200ml / 7fl oz bottles Poacher's Well Irish tonic water

In a large glass pitcher, combine Dingle Original Gin with the sliced lemon and lime. Arrange tall (Collins) glasses with lime wedges and ice nearby.
Allow guests to measure gin over ice to their own taste and top with tonic water.
Garnish with lime wedge.

CRANBERRY FISHBOWL

Makes 6 cocktails

2 limes, one sliced, one wedged
300ml / 10fl oz / 1¼ cup Dingle Distillery vodka
120g / 4¼oz / 1 cup fresh cranberries (frozen will suffice)
750ml / 24fl oz / 3 cups cranberry juice
prosecco
ice

In a deep jug, muddle lime slices with Dingle Distillery vodka. Let marinate for 30 minutes.
In a large glass pitcher, add fresh cranberries and strain vodka into this pitcher through a fine sieve.
Add cranberry juice and stir.
Allow guests to fill large balloon wine glasses (fishbowls) with ice and pour cocktail as they like.
Top with a splash of prosecco and garnish with lime wedge.

CUCUMBER COLLINS

Makes 6 cocktails

2 cucumbers, washed and sliced but kept separate
250ml / 8oz / 1 cup fresh lemon juice
250ml / 8oz / 1 cup gomme syrup (recipe on page 266)
500ml / 18fl oz / 2¼ cups Dingle Original Gin
1 lemon, sliced
ice
2 litres / 3½ pints / 8 cups soda water
mint sprigs for garnish

In a deep jug, muddle slices of one cucumber with lemon juice and gomme syrup. Add Dingle Original Gin and let marinate for 30 minutes.
In a glass pitcher, add second cucumber and lemon slices. Strain gin mixture through a fine mesh sieve into the pitcher and stir.
Allow guests to measure 120ml / 4oz into ice-filled tall (Collins) glasses. Top with soda and garnish with mint.

DINGLE DOG

Makes 6 cocktails

350ml / 12fl oz / 1⅓ cups Dingle Original Gin or Dingle Distillery vodka
550ml / 19fl oz / 2¼ cups freshly squeezed grapefruit juice
ice
Bar or kosher salt, or large-flaked sea salt

In a cocktail pitcher, mix gin (or vodka) and juice.
Moisten the rims of 6 lowball cocktail glasses and gently dip into salt. Tap off excess.
Three-quarter fill glasses with ice. Pour 150ml / 5¼fl oz / ⅔ cup of mixture into each glass and serve.

DINGLE FRENCH MARTINI

Makes 6 cocktails

350ml / 12fl oz / 1⅓ cups Dingle Distillery vodka
80ml / 3fl oz / ⅓ cup Chambord
350ml / 12fl oz / 1⅓ cups pineapple juice
ice
raspberries to garnish

In a cocktail pitcher, mix vodka, Chambord and pineapple juice.
To serve, fill a cocktail shaker with ice. Add double measure of vodka mixture.
Shake well.
Strain into cocktail (martini) glass. Garnish with raspberry.

DINGLE VESPER MARTINI

Makes 6 strong cocktails

350ml / 12fl oz / 1⅓ cups Dingle Original Gin
120ml / 4fl oz / ½ cup Dingle Distillery vodka
60ml / 2fl oz / ¼ cup Lillet Blanc
ice
lemon zest to garnish – 12 thick strips cut with a vegetable peeler

In a large glass pitcher, mix gin, vodka and Lillet.
Place one piece of zest in a cocktail shaker, fill with ice, add one double and one single measure of the gin mixture to the shaker. Shake vigorously for 10–15 seconds. Strain into a martini glass (or, even better, a champagne goblet) and garnish with twisted lemon zest.

FRENCH 75

Makes 6 cocktails

180ml / 6oz / ¾ cup fresh lemon juice
55g / ¼ cup caster (superfine) sugar
350ml / 12fl oz / 1⅓ cups Dingle Original Gin
ice
1 bottle champagne
orange half-moon slices for garnish

In a jug, mix lemon juice and sugar until dissolved. Add gin and mix well. Transfer to a glass pitcher.
Half-fill highball (Collins) glass with cracked ice. Add double measure of gin mixture and top with champagne.
Garnish with orange slice.

GIN & JUICE PUNCH

Makes 6 cocktails

350ml / 12fl oz / 1⅓ cups Dingle Original Gin
3 limes – 2 juiced, 1 cut into slices for garnish
2 lemons – 1 juiced, 1 cut into slices for garnish
1.5 litres / 2½ pints / 6 cups Sicilian-style lemonade (such as Lorina)
ice

In a punch bowl, mix gin with lemon and lime juice. Gently stir in Sicilian
lemonade. Top with slices of fruit and a few handfuls of ice.
Ladle into balloon (fishbowl) wine glasses.

GINITO

Makes 6 cocktails

2 lemons, sliced
250ml / 9fl oz / 1 cup gomme syrup (recipe on page 266)
500ml / 18oz / 2 cups Dingle Original Gin
1 handful fresh basil leaves plus more for garnish
ice
soda water
1 lemon, sliced for garnish

In a tall jug, muddle sliced lemons, syrup, gin and basil leaves together. Strain into
a pitcher. Place 1 leaf of basil in the bottom of a tall (highball/Collins) glass and fill
with ice.
Pour a double measure of the gin mixture into the glass, top with soda water and
garnish with another basil leaf and slice of lemon.

GRAPEFRUIT NEGRONI

Makes 6 cocktails

1 litre / 1¾ pints / 4 cups freshly squeezed grapefruit juice
350ml / 12fl oz / 1⅓ cups Dingle Original Gin
180ml / 6fl oz / ¾ cup sweet vermouth
80ml / 3fl oz / ⅓ cup Campari
6 strips grapefruit zest cut with vegetable peeler
cracked ice
6 grapefruit segments, peeled of their membrane

In a large glass pitcher, mix juice, gin, vermouth and Campari.
To serve, rub the inside of each of 6 lowball glasses with a strip of zest, reserve zest.
Fill glasses two-thirds full with cracked ice. Fill with juice and gin mixture.
Garnish with grapefruit segment and reserved zest.

HOP, SKIP & GO NAKED

Makes 6 cocktails

350ml / 12fl oz / 1⅓ cups Dingle Original Gin
180ml / 6fl oz / ¾ cup lemon juice
180ml / 6fl oz / ¾ cup lemon syrup (page 266)
350ml / 12fl oz / 1⅓ cups Porterhouse Herbrucker lager, Crean's lager or other hoppy lager
ice
lemon slices for garnish

In a large glass pitcher, stir gin, lemon juice and syrup together. Gently stir in the lager.
Invite your guests to fill a large white wine glass with ice and pour the cocktail to their taste. Garnish with lemon slice.

INVERTED LILLET MARTINI

Makes 6 cocktails

450ml / 16fl oz / 1¾ cups + 2 tbsp Lillet Blanc
80ml / 3fl oz / ⅓ cup Dingle Distillery vodka
ice
orange zest knots for garnish

In a tall glass pitcher, mix Lillet and vodka.
Into a cocktail shaker two thirds full of ice, add 90ml / 3¼fl oz Lillet / vodka mixture and shake well. Strain into a cocktail (martini) glass and garnish with orange zest knot.

~~~~~~

LIMONCELLO COLLINS

Makes 6 cocktails

350ml / 12fl oz / 1⅓ cups Dingle Original Gin
250ml / 9fl oz / 1 cup limoncello
cracked ice
soda water
lemon wedges for garnish

Mix gin and limoncello in a cocktail pitcher.
Two-thirds fill highball (Collins) cocktail glasses with cracked ice.
Add a double measure of gin mixture, top with soda water and stir gently. Garnish with lemon wedge.

MARMALADE MARTINI

Makes 6 cocktails

350ml / 12fl oz / 1⅓ cups Dingle Original Gin
80ml / 3fl oz / ⅓ cup Cointreau
80ml / 3fl oz / ⅓ cup fresh lime juice
2 tbsp Irish whiskey marmalade (or thick-cut marmalade)
ice
orange peel cut with channel knife

In a jug, mix all ingredients except garnish. Stir until marmalade is dissolved. Transfer to a cocktail pitcher.
To serve, fill a cocktail shaker with ice. Pour in a double measure of gin mixture and shake well. Strain into cocktail (martini) glass and garnish with orange twist.

MILLTOWN ROUNDABOUT

Makes 6 cocktails

80ml / 3fl oz / ⅓ cup fresh lemon juice
2 tbsp blackcurrant jam
450ml / 16fl oz / 1¾ cups + 2 tbsp Dingle Distillery vodka
ice
ginger ale
lemon zest knots for garnish

In a deep jug, muddle lemon juice and jam. Add vodka and allow to steep for 30 minutes. Strain into a tall glass pitcher.
Fill lowball glass with ice. Add double measure of vodka mixture and top with ginger ale.
Garnish with lemon zest.

PASSION FRUIT CAIPIROSKA

Makes 6 cocktails

3 passion fruit, cut in half
3 limes, cut into quarters
6 tbsp brown sugar
60ml / 2fl oz / ¼ cup simple syrup (page 266)
350ml / 12fl oz / 1⅓ cups Dingle Distillery vodka
crushed ice

Set out six lowball cocktail glasses.
Into each glass, scoop the flesh from one half of a passion fruit. Add two lime quarters, 1 tablespoon brown sugar and 2½ teaspoons syrup.
Muddle the ingredients very well in each glass.
To serve, half fill glass with crushed ice, add double measure of vodka and stir well.
Top with additional crushed ice to fill the glass.

PINK GIN

Makes 6 cocktails

18 drops Angostura (or orange) bitters
350ml / 12fl oz / 1⅓ cups Dingle Original Gin
ice – optional

Line up six lowball cocktail glasses and place three drops of bitters in each. Swirl the bitters around and pour remainder into a cocktail pitcher. Measure gin into the pitcher and swirl to mix.
Invite guests to pour a double measure into the prepared glasses.
A cube of ice is optional but purists will sneer at the thought.

PROSECCO COCKTAIL

Makes 6 cocktails

2 tbsp Angostura bitters
6 white sugar cubes
1–2 bottles of dry Italian prosecco
orange twists for garnish

Pour the bitters into a small dish. Dip sugar cubes into bitters and drop one into each of six tall champagne flutes.
Fill glasses with prosecco.
Garnish with orange twists.

RYAN'S DOWNFALL

Makes 12 cocktails

350ml / 12oz / 1⅓ cups freshly squeezed lime juice
350ml / 12oz / 1⅓ cups lime syrup (page 266)
350ml / 12oz / 1⅓ cups Dingle Original Gin
ice
soda water
lime slices for garnish

In a large pitcher, mix juice, syrup and gin together in equal parts and refrigerate to chill. This base mixture can be stored in freezer (thaw before use).
In tall champagne flutes add one double measure of the cocktail mixture (this can be done before the guests arrive). Add two cubes of ice and top with soda water. Garnish with lime slice.
Ryan's Downfall is fairly low in alcohol so I've included the recipe for two per person. Extra base can be frozen if not used.

SEASIDE ROYALE

Makes 6 cocktails

3 limes, cut into quarters
60ml / 2fl oz / ¼ cup gomme syrup (page 266)
300ml / ½ pint / 1¼ cups Dingle Original Gin
champagne
mint to garnish

In a tall jug, muddle lime wedges with syrup to extract juice and flavour. Pour in gin and allow to steep for 10 minutes.
Strain through a fine sieve into a cocktail pitcher.
Three-quarters fill a tallboy (Collins) cocktail glass with ice. Add 60ml / 2fl oz / ¼ cup gin mixture and top with champagne.
Garnish with mint.

~~~~~~

SINGAPORE GIN SLING

Makes 6 cocktails

250ml / 9oz / 1 cup Dingle Original Gin
80ml / 3fl oz / ⅓ cup Cherry Heering
45ml / 1½fl oz / 3 tbsp Cointreau
45ml / 1½fl oz / 3 tbsp Benedictine
750ml / 24fl oz / 3 cups pineapple juice
80ml / 3fl oz / ⅓ cup fresh lime juice
60ml / 2fl oz / ¼ cup Grenadine
6 dashes Angostura bitters
ice
6 cocktail cherries and 6 pineapple wedge for garnish

Mix all ingredients except ice and garnish in a large pitcher.
Have guests fill white wine glasses two-thirds full with cracked ice and pour a 210ml / 7fl oz serving of the mixture into each glass as guests arrive.
Garnish with pineapple wedge and cocktail cherry.

THE WEST KERRY HEDGEROW

Makes 6 cocktails

6 small sprigs rosemary
12 organic fuchsia flowers
18 juniper berries
6 blackberries
1 lemon cut into 6 slices
1 lime cut into 6 slices
2 grapefruit slices cut into thirds
ice
6 bottles Fever-Tree Indian tonic
360ml / 12fl oz / 1⅓ cups Dingle Original Gin

In each of six balloon (fishbowl) glasses, place one sprig rosemary, two fuchsia flowers, three juniper berries, one blackberry, and a slice each of lemon, lime and grapefruit.

Add 60ml / 2fl oz / ¼ cup gin.

When guests arrive, fill glasses halfway with ice and pour in tonic.

NON-ALCOHOLIC COCKTAILS

It's important to have a selection of non-alcoholic beverages on hand when planning a dinner party. Juices (sparkling or still), soft drinks and mixers are an important part of any host's bar.

PINEAPPLE GINGER FIZZ

Serves 6

1 litre / 1¾ pints / 4 cups ginger ale, chilled
1 litre / 1¾ pints / 4 cups pineapple juice, chilled
1 orange, thinly sliced
1 piece (5cm / 2in) fresh stem ginger, thinly sliced
12 fresh basil leaves, destemmed
12 fresh mint leaves, destemmed, plus more for garnish

In a large pitcher, combine the ginger ale and pineapple juice. Top with orange slices, ginger, basil, and mint.
Pour into tall glasses filled with crushed ice and garnish with mint leaves.

SPARKLING LEMONADE

Serves 6

350ml / 12fl oz / 1⅓ cups freshly squeezed lemon juice – pips removed
350ml / 12fl oz / 1⅓ cups lemon simple syrup (page 266)
700ml / 24fl oz / 3 cups sparkling water
6 lemon slices for garnish

Two-thirds fill balloon wine glasses with crushed ice.
Add 60ml / 2fl oz each of lemon juice and lemon syrup to each glass and stir.
Top glasses with sparkling water, stirring gently as you pour.
Garnish with lemon slice.

SPARKLING PEAR PUNCH

Serves 6
240ml / 8fl oz / 1 cup pear juice
juice of 1 lemon
60g / 2oz / ¼ cup sugar
1 litre / 32fl oz ginger ale
6 thin slices fresh pear for garnish

Pour pear juice into large punch bowl and add lemon juice. Stir in sugar to dissolve. Gently mix in ginger ale.
Place slices of pear into fancy glasses and fill with ice. Ladle punch into glasses.

SYRUPS

SIMPLE SYRUP (WITH VARIATIONS)

200g / 7oz / 1 cup granulated sugar
240ml / 8fl oz / 1 cup water

In a heavy, straight-sided pot, dissolve sugar in half the water. Use remaining water to wash down sides of pot so no crystals remain stuck to the sides.
Heat sugar water over medium–high heat until boiling. Can be covered for the first few minutes to encourage steam to wash down the sides of the pot.
Cool completely and store in an airtight container in the refrigerator for up to a week.

Variations

Lime Syrup
Using a vegetable peeler, peel the zest from three limes.
Once syrup has boiled, stir to make sure all sugar is dissolved. Remove from heat, add zest, cover and leave overnight. Strain and chill.

Lemon Syrup
Using a vegetable peeler, peel the zest from three lemons (yellow part only, no white).
Once syrup has boiled, stir to make sure all sugar is dissolved. Remove from heat, add zest, cover and leave overnight. Strain and chill.

GOMME SYRUP

30g / 1oz / 1 tbsp food-grade gum arabic
60ml / 2fl oz / ¼ cup hot water
250g / 9oz / 1¼ cups sugar
120ml / 4fl oz / ½ cup water

Heat water to near boiling, add gum arabic and allow it to stand until it is 'dissolved'. This could take a few hours (or more). The gum will swell and soak up the water to become a sticky paste.
Separately, dissolve sugar in water and bring to a slow boil. Add gum arabic mixture and return to a boil for two minutes, stirring constantly.
Use a spoon to remove any foam on the surface.
Cool and strain through a fine sieve. Store in an airtight container in the refrigerator for up to 1 week.

ACKNOWLEDGEMENTS

As in their own kitchens, the stars of this book are the featured chefs (and their food). I cannot thank them enough for suffering unnumbered calls, e-mails and meetings to get their stories and recipes right. Like food from those kitchens, however, there is a broad supporting cast who have made it possible to deliver this 'plate' to your table.

It was The Collins Press who tossed out the first seeds when they asked if I'd be interested in writing a book about the storied foods of the Dingle Peninsula. That was a Thursday and they had my proposal on their desk on Monday morning. What an honour (and great good fun) to write this book. The entire publishing staff have, once again, made the process a joy.

Mary Ferriter, John Sheehy, and Artie Clifford - from The Dingle Distillery, The Dingle Food Festival and Blas na hÉireann respectively – saw the potential in the work and marshalled sponsorship requests onto appropriate desks.

Kristen Jensen's deft hand with metric conversions (and making sense of my American spellings) was, once again for me, invaluable.

Jette Virdi styled our food and properties exquisitely, Joanne Murphy photographed the dishes so well you can smell it and Elaine Kennedy captured each chef's unique personality effortlessly … and patiently. No matter how good the recipes and writing, *Dingle Dinners* would be nothing but a pamphlet were it not for their talents and passions.

Dingle Town itself plays a major role in the book and, now, in the life of my family. We have been welcomed and included by Dingle and it's surrounds and we are most grateful. I hope this book represents you well to all corners of the world.

The complement of chefs who have inspired me throughout my career and the writing of *Dingle Dinners* is too long to list, but I would be remiss if I didn't call out Dale Jakowski, Michel LeBorgne, Jack Wich, Kathy Casey, and Nevin Maguire. And Nevin for agreeing to write the forward, cannot be thanked enough.

Finally, my wife, Caryn, has been supportive throughout the birthing process of this work in a way that only writers can understand, only the most fortunate ever experience and of which only saints (and surely not chefs) are worthy. Thank you, Petal.

INDEX